NO ONE PLANNED THIS
HOW PLATFORMS REWIRED ENTERTAINMENT

DARREN CROSS

Disclaimer: This is a work of nonfiction based on the author's experiences and research. Some names and identifying details may have been changed or aggregated to protect privacy.

Copyright © 2026 Darren Cross

All rights reserved. No part of this book may be reproduced or used in any manner without the prior written permission of the copyright owner, except for the use of brief quotations in a review.

To request permissions, contact: permissions@nooneplannedthis.com

Hardcover: ISBN 979-8-9931752-0-1

Paperback: ISBN 979-8-9931752-1-8

Ebook: ISBN 979-8-9931752-2-5

Audiobook: ISBN 979-8-9931752-3-2

Library of Congress Control Number: 2025920624

First hardcover, paperback, ebook, and audiobook editions February 2026.

Publisher: dca — Los Angeles, California

Published in association with Cordurouy Books — Hermosa Beach, California

Cover design by David Ter-Avanesyan/Ter33Design LLC

Printed in the United States of America.

nooneplannedthis.com

For Monica, Tina, and Lucas—who make all of this matter, and for Lucas's generation, the first to grow up fully inside the world this book is trying to explain.

CONTENTS_

Preface	1
Prologue: Signal Over Noise	5

PART 1
ATTENTION

1 Beatles? Or Monkees?	23
2 Building Without Permission	35
3 The Myth of the Creator Middle Class	53
4 Creators as Machines	71

PART 2
POWER

5 When YouTube Becomes TV	85
6 Who Really Owns the Audience?	97
7 Infrastructure Is the New Star System	111
8 One Is the Loneliest Number	123

PART 3
AFFILIATION

9 What If We Put the Audience First?	137
10 Channels, Not Shows	147
11 Identity Over Interface	163
12 Ritual & Return	179
Epilogue: The Next Signal	191
Acknowledgments	201
About the Author	203

PREFACE_

THE CREATOR ECONOMY wasn't supposed to happen—not like this, not at this scale, not with this much power in the hands of people who, a decade ago, weren't considered legitimate. Not by studios. Not by platforms. Least of all by advertisers.

But it did.

A recent Deloitte study confirmed what was already visible in the data: Gen Z now prefers creator-driven video over traditional TV and film, and Gen Alpha is growing up with creators not as an alternative but as their first storytellers, entertainers, and role models. This isn't a trend line, it's a generational reset. The legitimacy shift happened through audience preference, not institutional validation. Creators won because their content feels close, speaks the language of their audience, and thrives on intimacy and immediacy. Where traditional media relies on polish and distance, creator content turned audiences into participants who respond, remix, and reframe—turning content into culture in real time.

I've spent twenty years inside the shift: at Wedbush analyzing Netflix before "streaming" meant anything; at Morgan Freeman/Intel-backed ClickStar as films went day-and-date; at Fandango as the internet went everywhere; at Disney-acquired Maker Studios as creators became economic forces. I spotted signals, convinced stakeholders, and helped get products to market—often in layers no one was watching.

That includes the messy early phases of what we now call the creator economy: before the big exits, before creator-led brands—back when platforms paid for content without understanding creators. When media companies tried to manufacture virality. When social video was a side project, not the foundation.

It wasn't a phase, and it still isn't.

This book is a signal scan, an attempt to map the deeper transformation still underway. It was developed in real time as the ground shifted beneath us—in boardrooms and classrooms, and in the behavior of my own son and his friends as they moved effortlessly between YouTube, TikTok, Twitch, and whatever comes next. I first saw the signal in places that seemed minor at the time—a film available in theaters and online the same day, smartphones making the internet always-on, YouTubers landing major book deals and topping bestseller lists.

The conversations revealed patterns. The patterns pointed to something bigger than creator monetization or influencer culture: a reconfiguration of how culture spreads, how audiences form, and how value flows, through the invisible architecture underneath platforms, driven by infrastructure that enables identity and ritual, not just more content.

What follows is a framework, a way to read the signals and act on them, without pretending to predict the future. We'll trace the rise of platforms and the hollowing of the creator middle class; the shift from algorithmic factories to ambient networks; from monetization tricks to identity design, from content to infrastructure.

The through line is simple: we're not at the end of something. We're at the beginning.

The creator economy wasn't the destination. It was the first signal.

If we learn to read it, we might glimpse what comes next.

PROLOGUE: SIGNAL OVER NOISE_

IN 2004, I was a junior equity analyst at Wedbush Securities in Los Angeles, working under Michael Pachter. Getting there hadn't been a straight line. I'd started as a musician—graduating from Musicians Institute, playing around LA in clubs like The Viper Room and the Troubadour—but after watching talented peers struggle to make ends meet, I pivoted: first to law school, then business school, and eventually to a job where I built spreadsheets instead of playing late-night sets.

When I started with Michael, I was learning the job under Ed, Michael's senior associate, supporting coverage of video game publishers like EA, Activision, and THQ. Ed retained lead associate status on gaming publishers, but I inherited names outside the gaming vertical, including Blockbuster—under Michael, who led coverage of the company. Between the two of us, we knew Blockbuster's business about as well as anyone outside the company could. Then Michael handed me a new name: Netflix, a fast-growing DVD-by-mail company, publicly traded but still niche, competing with Blockbuster's profit engine of ubiquitous stores and late fees.

I was supposed to analyze Netflix as a DVD rental competitor to Blockbuster. But my path to that analyst desk had given me outsider wiring that would prove essential.

Before Wedbush, I'd spent four years at Aerospace Service & Controls, later ASC Process Systems, founded by a former bandmate, Dave. We made PC-based control systems using thermocouples for real-time, closed-loop feedback during advanced carbon-fiber curing—displacing PLCs that could only follow recipes and required cutting physical samples after the fact. Our system streamed process history and closed the loop in real time. Quality was instrumented, not inferred. Our clients were Boeing, Lockheed, Northrop Grumman, and EADS (now Airbus).

I stayed four years. We were successful, but it wasn't mine and it wasn't inspiring. Law school had been like a liberal-arts degree on steroids. The MBA was more functional—useful, but not where I wanted to live. Equity research seemed like the right application of the degree, and less grinding than consulting. Those detours—law, industrial software, business school—gave me an outsider lens that later mapped to creator culture: people who won't fit the Disney or Comcast mold. That restlessness is why I saw Netflix differently; I wasn't optimizing for Wall Street's ladder, I was testing different values against the same data.

Growing up in indie culture, I'd learned the best stuff lived in the margins. Tower and Blockbuster carried what could move units; the discoveries happened at record stores like Amoeba and Aron's, video shops like Le Video and Vidiots—found through friends, clerks, and luck. Access took work most people wouldn't do. In music and movies, the hits were often formats perfected for replication. I wanted the pieces that refused the template—singular, surprising. And I knew millions of people shared specific tastes that mainstream distribution couldn't serve efficiently.

I'd always had a strong sense for "this is like that" across products, industries, and disciplines. What all those detours did was refine that intuitive facility with analogy. I could hear source inspirations in music, see narrative patterns jump from books to films to completely different mediums. While other analysts stayed in their silos, I kept connecting dots—seeing how the dynamics reshaping music distribution would inevitably hit video, how behavioral patterns in one technology adoption predicted another. That cross-pollination, plus my indie sensibility and outsider psychology, meant I wasn't analyzing Netflix as a logistics company. I was watching software displace entrenched systems by delivering what customers needed —the same pattern I'd seen at ASC.

I'd watched the music industry evolve in real time. Back then, every step was friction. People wanted access to new music immediately, but the industry forced them into entire albums from physical stores during business hours. Napster was illegal, but it delivered what people wanted:

any song, instantly, from home. The industry called it theft. I saw it as human nature finally getting the technology it needed. The disruption was swift and brutal: unlimited digital catalogs, rampant piracy, and a vacuum created by labels' reluctance to embrace legitimate digital distribution.

The shift was emerging in video. To build the coverage model, I studied adoption curves for cable TV, the VCR, and the internet. Each moved faster than the last once it delivered what audiences craved: choice and control over their entertainment. As the pipes got better, behavior followed.

The prevailing wisdom said people wanted to own content. My read was different. When people bought DVDs, they thought they were buying movies—but they were really buying plastic, with limited rights to what was on it. Digital stripped away even that illusion. The value was never in possession; it was in the experience. And if experience was what mattered, access would always beat ownership.

That generalist background and comfort with analogy is what let me see Netflix clearly. Their revenue-sharing deals with major studios meant they paid per rental for blockbusters, but they could buy deep-catalog titles outright and amortize that cost across unlimited rentals. Economically, Netflix often had better unit economics on owned titles than on revenue-shared new releases. Cinematch, their early recommendation system, frequently nudged viewing toward titles that were always available, and often more profitable. Netflix could feature an independent documentary right next to blockbusters in personalized recommendations. The system made money surfacing what mainstream distribution had buried.

This wasn't just clever logistics. Netflix was solving a problem I understood viscerally: access to culture that lived outside the mainstream. When you remove distribution constraints and make discovery effortless, micro-audiences become economically viable. But this went beyond economics—it was about validating the existence of all the people who'd felt like outsiders to mainstream culture, who'd had to work to find what they wanted. Netflix was saying that their taste mattered, that there was economic value in serving them, that they didn't have to settle for what mainstream distribution deemed worthy of shelf space. The algorithm became a kind of cultural democracy, where popularity could emerge organically from the bottom up rather than being dictated from the top down.

The streaming transition would amplify this exponentially. Physical constraints had forced Netflix to make inventory decisions about which obscure titles to stock. Unlimited digital shelf space meant they could serve any niche, no matter how specific, as long as an audience existed. Streaming would remove the last big friction—no pressing discs, no convincing retailers, no fighting for shelf space.

Netflix already understood this. The DVD-by-mail model was just the bridge. Rentals had moved people past the need to own, but streaming would erase the remaining friction: no getting off the couch, no planning days ahead, no waiting for the red envelope. No stockouts, your picks available instantly. Streaming would turn movie-watching from a planned activity into an impulse decision. Once that experience became seamless, it wasn't just competitive, it was obvious.

Independent filmmakers who could never get theatrical distribution could now reach their people directly. Foreign films that would never make it to American multiplexes could find their niche audiences. Documentarians, experimental filmmakers, anyone making work for passionate micro-communities rather than mass audiences—Netflix was creating economic opportunity for them. Soon after, platforms like YouTube would remove the gate entirely, letting anyone with a camera find an audience without asking permission.

This was the beginning of what we now call the creator economy, in which makers could reach audiences without asking permission from traditional gatekeepers. Netflix was just the first major platform to prove that technology could make these connections profitable at scale. But the implications went far beyond video. The same dynamics would reshape music, publishing, education, journalism—virtually every creative field.

My valuation implied a Buy—not because the near-term financials were compelling, but because the behavioral shift was coming. The adoption curve was bending toward on-demand access. Streaming wasn't a question of if, only when. Netflix, by owning the customer relationship and building the infrastructure early, was positioned to lead the transition. Michael, as lead analyst, owned the rating; his valuation supported a Sell, and that's the call we published.

Michael's model reflected legitimate concerns. He worried about cannibalizing Netflix's profitable DVD business before streaming revenue could replace it. The licensing economics were brutal: if streaming took off too quickly, the costs could swamp them. We'd already run the numbers: heavy users, "whales," could push the DVD model into the red if they rented more than six or seven discs a month, especially for new releases where Netflix paid dearly per rental. Streaming those same customers could mean paying licensing fees on every view, without the physical constraint that kept DVD costs in check.

He was focused on near-term execution risks: two business models cannibalizing each other, broadband infrastructure still patchy, cash burn during the transition. And he was right to worry. Timing was everything. The DVDs were funding the streaming buildup—but streaming threatened to kill the DVD business before it could replace the revenue.

He also understood something else I didn't fully grasp at the time: how equity research really works. A Sell, especially a contrarian one, gets attention. When we initiated, we were the only firm with a formal Sell; headlines followed. That was smart, not cynical.

We were analyzing the same company through different lenses. Michael saw Netflix as a successful DVD-by-mail company pivoting to broadband delivery at a time when broadband wasn't terribly broad, a risky transition full of execution challenges. I looked at the longer-term evolution of content distribution and monetization, focused on where behavioral shifts were heading regardless of short-term constraints. We weren't contradicting each other; we were operating on different time horizons. His perspective was grounded in immediate realities; mine was tracking inevitable patterns. Both were valid.

What I carried forward wasn't a better stock call—it was a framework for perspective. That same pattern sense, plus my comfort operating outside specialist silos, is what let me recognize when human behavior was ready to abandon an old system for a new one. I'd recognized the same behavioral shift that had gutted the music industry, but this time, I understood what to look for. When behavior moves, infrastructure follows, and new rooms get built.

That realization—that the same behavioral forces reshaping music were about to hit film and TV—was when I first understood what infrastructure meant. Infrastructure wasn't about pipes or bandwidth. It was about removing friction between people and what they wanted. Infrastructure didn't just move content; it rewired access and changed who got to participate. And once that shift started, it wouldn't stop with video.

ClickStar would teach me how slow and complicated that "inevitable" can be when you try to make it real.

When I joined ClickStar in September 2005—an early experiment in internet-first movie distribution co-founded by Morgan Freeman and backed by Intel Capital—the energy was electric. We positioned it as an anti-Napster move: help Hollywood avoid the music industry's collapse by embracing digital distribution before piracy forced their hand. The idea was audacious: give people the ability to purchase or rent movies online, day-and-date with their theatrical release. In 2005, that felt like science fiction. The pitch was simple: give people legal access to what they want, when they want it, or watch them find illegal ways to get it. I'd seen this movie before.

For that era, what we pulled off was groundbreaking: several day-and-date theatrical-and-digital releases that cracked decades of entrenched windowing—despite cool studio caution, hostile theater chains, and a slate of films that, while strong, weren't built to be the year's biggest box-office draws. Each release required complex negotiations with theater chains, distributors, and studio executives fiercely protective of existing revenue models. On the ground, I negotiated *Al Franken: God Spoke* directly with Frazer Pennebaker, visited Janus/Criterion to encourage them to lead a channel, and met with Ric Burns about exploring a flagship relationship for our documentary vertical.

Independent and documentary filmmakers were focused on something more basic than windowing theory: discovery. The home-entertainment window was dominated by the majors, and they were unsure their films would be findable or watchable at home even if the tech worked.

But we learned the hard way that being right about the future doesn't guarantee success in the present. Broadband wasn't there. Most households were still limping along on DSL; buffering was expected, and a successful progressive download felt like a win. The devices meant to deliver it? Most never existed while ClickStar was alive, and the ones that did fell far short of their promise.

Beyond the tech, Hollywood's model wouldn't budge. Napster had put them on alert, they could see piracy coming for them too, but always from a safe distance. Release windows stayed fixed: theatrical, then pay-per-view, then DVD, then cable. Each was a dependable revenue stream. The executives running those divisions were personally incentivized to keep it that way. We weren't just fighting the thesis—we were fighting the comp plan.

Most major studios were happy to take ClickStar's substantial minimum guarantees—it was low-risk money for them, guaranteed upfront regardless of how digital performed. Disney was the notable holdout, unwilling to participate. Independents approached it differently. They had less leverage for big MGs but more to gain from what digital access might unlock, and they were willing to experiment with revenue-share models and non-traditional distribution to reach audiences gatekeepers had long ignored.

ClickStar, despite its intent, technical achievements, and the talent it attracted, became a casualty of timing and inertia. The company struggled financially and eventually shut down, unable to bridge the gap between future-facing tech and the market realities of 2006–2007. The tech worked, within the limits of that day's tech, and the read on direction was right. Why use 90 percent of the signal coming into your home for cable TV—every channel, all the time—when that same pipe could carry the internet, where you pull what you want when you want it? The future was obvious: most of your broadband would be for the internet, not cable.

The signal was real. The infrastructure just wasn't there to receive it.

When I joined Fandango in 2007, the internet was still a desktop-bound experience. Web services assumed users were at home or in an office, behind a big screen with reliable broadband. Phones were complicated, underpowered devices with tiny screens and slow data that made basic browsing frustrating.

Fandango's leadership acknowledged mobile as a growing segment but treated it as a minor extension of the core web business—handled through carrier "walled-garden" portals that wouldn't disrupt revenue from web traffic, advertising, and ticket fees. Like Blockbuster, Fandango was optimizing for what was working, not what was coming.

The company had other priorities. Sophisticated web advertising products were generating solid, predictable revenue—pop-under ads that persisted after users left a page, banner placements, rich-media integrations that commanded premium rates from studios. We also earned substantial income from post-transaction marketing partnerships with Webloyalty and Affinion. Browser-only data-pass deals (later scrutinized by the FTC) didn't translate to apps. There was understandable reluctance to risk them for a mobile strategy with unclear returns and real technical challenges.

Then the summer of 2008 brought the iPhone 3G, a shift that put real computing and connectivity in people's pockets, not just another upgrade. The touch interface, reliable internet, and the App Store unleashed a gold rush. Thousands of apps appeared seemingly overnight, many built by independents scraping websites to create new mobile experiences.

For Fandango, that wave created both opportunity and pressure. Independent developers began scraping our showtimes and pulling trailers, building mobile movie apps that threatened to bypass our site entirely. We suddenly found ourselves racing well-funded startups like Flixster, while our traditional competitor MovieTickets.com scrambled alongside us.

It felt like late '90s broadband, only faster. This time, computing power and internet access would live in people's pockets, changing when and how entertainment decisions got made. I became convinced this shift would favor utility services like Fandango—transforming it from a planning tool at home into an impulse-enabling service you could access anywhere.

The value proposition was simple. Instead of looking up showtimes before leaving the house, we could reach users at the exact moment of intent. Picture it: you're out with friends on a Saturday night, standing on a street corner, debating what to do next. Someone pulls out a phone and asks, "What's playing? When does it start? Where's the closest theater? Can we get tickets right now?" Our app could answer all of it instantly—bridging a fleeting impulse to a completed transaction.

This was commerce and attention capture built around the new behavior mobile created, not a traditional content play. We weren't entertaining users; we were serving immediate needs: What are you planning to see? With whom? Where? When? That intersection of consumer behavior and digital infrastructure fascinated me then, and it still does.

Internally, product, marketing, and sales saw the

mobile opportunity quickly once the iPhone showed what was possible. The real challenge was convincing the C-suite to embrace a mobile-first strategy that would hit the top line. Existing models were working. Post-transaction marketing partnerships generated substantial income, web ad relationships were profitable and predictable, and mobile apps would inherently eliminate the post-transaction revenue entirely—those data-pass mechanisms only worked in desktop browsers. Sales compensation and quarterly targets were tied to desktop metrics. Mobile adoption wasn't just a product call; it demanded top-line courage and meant walking away from revenue models that were already ethically questionable.

The C-suite resistance wasn't irrational. Why risk profitable relationships and steady revenue for a mobile strategy that was still theoretical? At first, the iPhone was one device from one manufacturer, and there was real uncertainty about whether mobile commerce would develop quickly enough to justify the investment and the immediate loss of lucrative desktop income.

But the iPhone's meteoric rise, and the broader smartphone boom, made the case undeniable. Mobile wasn't just changing how people interacted with Fandango; it was changing how they made entertainment decisions, shifting from planned choices at home to spontaneous, location-based choices in real time. That created new opportunities for impulse purchases and last-minute decisions that didn't exist in the desktop-only era.

The lesson was clear: frictionless access to services, delivered at the point of need and intent, can transform established models, and eventually overcome organizational resistance. Getting big organizations to embrace that transformation before it's obviously necessary? That's the hard part.

While I was still at Fandango, running strategy and business development, I encountered something that reshaped my understanding of what an audience could be. In 2010, Oliver Luckett approached me from DigiSynd—Disney's quietly acquired digital outfit. On the surface, they managed Disney's presence on Facebook and YouTube. What Oliver pitched was different: a distributed content campaign for *Toy Story 3* that would run natively inside social feeds—not as ads, but as shareable, culturally fluent posts—content that spread because it fit the feed.

I was in immediately. Group viewing sparked through social sharing meant real ticket sales. Group buying made Fandango indispensable on opening weekends. And it deepened our relationship with Disney—a studio whose favor was worth earning. I led internally, advocating for the campaign and aligning the right teams. This was a behavior shift, not a marketing exercise. But brand dollars moved slowly because social couldn't be measured like traditional advertising. We weren't fighting impact—we were fighting budget inertia.

What DigiSynd was building wasn't traditional digital media. It was an early playbook for influencing at scale, platform-native persuasion, not promotion. Working with Oliver was my first real exposure to distributed media strategy: not placing content around culture, but embedding it inside culture. He brought the muscle memory of political organizing and behavioral psychology to entertainment. He was building a new playbook.

I didn't know it yet, but that was the beginning of a throughline that would define the next phase of my career. DigiSynd was absorbed quietly into Disney. Oliver wasn't done. A few years later, he took everything he'd learned and started something new—a company that didn't just work with influence, but tried to industrialize it.

PART 1
ATTENTION_

Every shift in media starts the same way. Not with a press release. Not with a gadget. With a change in what people do. They look elsewhere. They stop watching. They start tapping. And for a while, no one notices.

Behavior moves first, quietly, and everything else scrambles to catch up. Infrastructure bends. Platforms pivot. Business models rewire. It all begins with the way attention moves.

The chapters ahead track those shifts as signals, not footnotes. Early digital platforms turned attention into something selectable and interactive. The jump from linear programming to algorithmic feeds rewrote our relationship to time, choice, and engagement. A new kind of user emerged: active, self-curating, trained by invisible systems of distribution and reward.

As those systems matured, they tilted the table— funneling attention and payouts toward the few and reshaping who could win and how. Pressure turned creators into machines, optimizing for algorithms over expression. Attention became the currency of the media economy. Everyone learned to chase it. Few stopped to ask what it cost.

These chapters examine that pivot between eras, what it feels like to live through a platform shift before it has a name. From early signals of disruption to factory systems of production. From the illusion of a creator middle class to the reality of power laws and platform dependency.

The transformation wasn't planned; the patterns were predictable. They're still playing out.

1 BEATLES? OR MONKEES?

IN ENTERTAINMENT, there have always been two paths to stardom. One is manufactured: constructed in boardrooms, polished on soundstages, engineered for mass appeal. The other emerges organically from garages, clubs, and bedrooms, raw, unpredictable, magnetic.

The entertainment industry's early attempts to channel and monetize the chaotic energy of social media were a classic case of aiming for The Monkees when what the digital landscape needed was The Beatles. It was a misreading of the signals coming from a new generation of digital natives—an insistence on imposing old logic onto a new medium.

Even the more forward-thinking Hollywood players— those who saw platforms like Twitter, YouTube, and Instagram not as threats but as opportunity—still applied the same playbook they'd always used. The idea was to industrialize influence: build systems, script personas, and polish content to create scalable digital fame. But the ecosystem wasn't interested in polish or celebrities. It was craving something born of unexpected connection and raw expression.

The difference wasn't subtle. It was structural. Platforms weren't just new distribution pipes for old entertainment. They were generative systems. They didn't reward polish or pedigree; they rewarded behavior. And that behavior didn't look anything like a network television rollout. It looked like chaos. It looked like a teenager posting from their bedroom with no script and no filter. It looked like someone playing Minecraft for four hours with their mic on and a live chat rolling. And it worked because it was real, not sloppy. The Monkees metaphor captures this distinction perfectly—The Monkees were assembled for television, controlled from the top down, while The Beatles were a phenomenon that no one could have scripted.

And that's the mistake we repeatedly made in those early years: we thought it could be scripted.

I saw these early misreadings up close, especially at theAudience, a social media agency co-founded by Sean Parker, Oliver Luckett, and Ari Emanuel, where we tried to bring structure and strategy to a system that was inherently unscripted.

Oliver brought me in to tackle two things: help optimize their existing celebrity commerce work—they knew Fandango's purchase flow was industry-leading and wanted that expertise applied to turning social posts into actual sales—and explore whether crowdfunding could work for unknown music artists, using what established acts were doing successfully on services like PledgeMusic, Kickstarter, and Indiegogo.

The crowdfunding success stories all looked the same. Amanda Palmer raised over a million for her album. Steve Vai funded his documentary. Ben Folds Five got their record made after their label said no. But they weren't building audiences—they were cashing in on audiences they'd spent decades building. Palmer had the Dresden Dolls fanbase. Vai was already a guitar legend. Ben Folds had nearly two decades of earned affection. Oliver's idea was that we could replicate their success with artists nobody had ever heard of—as if connection could be manufactured.

They built editorial calendars for Adam Sandler's Twitter feed, ghostwrote "spontaneous" posts for Pearl Jam, managed Bob Marley's estate on social media—trying to make a dead reggae legend feel current on platforms that didn't exist when he was alive—and worked with Mark Wahlberg, Pitbull, and others, getting approval before blasting out optimized tweets and status updates.

The approach worked, at least financially. Their campaign for *Spring Breakers* helped the movie gross more than $30 million worldwide with minimal promotional costs, leveraging the social network power of Selena Gomez, Vanessa Hudgens, and James Franco. But even successful campaigns felt hollow, they were manufacturing moments that were supposed to feel organic.

We championed a simple principle internally: social engagement should drive purchases. We kept trying to apply Fandango-style funnel optimization to celebrity client workflows, but turning "Hey Cleveland, who's coming to the show?" into conversions required a level of platform fluency most established acts didn't have.

And for a while, in terms of raw follower counts and impressions, it seemed to work. The numbers were there. But beneath the surface, something else was happening.

While theAudience's teams were managing feeds for A-listers and legacy acts, a new generation of creators was rising—individuals with no industry ties, no traditional fame, and no intention of waiting for anyone's permission.

The shift from text-based social to visual and video platforms created new creative possibilities that established media couldn't easily colonize. Each platform evolution, from Twitter's 140 characters to YouTube's unlimited video to Instagram's visual storytelling, created fresh territory where authenticity had a head start over manufacturing.

The first real wave started on YouTube. By 2012, while we were scripting tweets for established stars, YouTubers were building massive audiences from scratch based not on production value or professional polish, but on raw presence. They were funny, vulnerable, awkward, and undeniably authentic. They made things up on the fly, talked directly to the camera as if they were FaceTiming a close friend, got personal about their lives, and embraced the weird, the niche, the unconventional. And people couldn't look away.

What made this different from traditional media wasn't just the lower barriers to entry, it was the intimacy. Television created celebrities you admired from a distance. YouTube created personalities you felt you knew personally. The comment sections weren't fan mail; they were ongoing conversations. Creators responded, remembered regular viewers, built inside jokes that spanned months of uploads. This was participation, not consumption.

Instagram's real transformation came after Facebook's 2012 acquisition, when the social giant poured resources into what had been a simple photo-sharing app. By 2013, it had evolved into an entirely different language of influence built around aspirational but personal imagery, not just YouTube content reformatted for photos.

By 2013, Vine introduced a radically compressed canvas: six seconds, looping endlessly. Within that constraint, a generation of creators pioneered a language that was chaotic and irresistibly funny. They weren't polished or packaged—they were unfiltered, often weird, and intensely personal. Vine didn't just introduce short-form video; it cracked open a new kind of intimacy between creator and audience.

What these early creators understood intuitively was that platforms weren't just tools for distribution—they were environments that rewarded specific behaviors. And those behaviors had nothing to do with traditional production values.

Production logic is a pipeline: develop, package, market, release. It exists to make outcomes predictable, budgets locked, calendars set, approvals secured, risk contained. Platform logic is a loop: publish, observe, adapt, repeat. It exists to make outcomes discoverable, tight feedback cycles in public, learning accrued in increments, momentum earned rather than forecast.

The difference shows up first in time. Pipelines wait for greenlights while loops move now, and where a pipeline defers contact with the audience until everything is "ready," a loop treats contact with the audience as the work itself.

It also shows up in how conviction is formed. Production logic builds certainty upstream, treatments, comps, research, internal consensus. Platform logic builds certainty downstream, performance signals, retention curves, return-viewer patterns. In a pipeline, you argue the case for what will work; in a loop, you demonstrate the trend that is already improving.

Economically, the pipeline front-loads cost and reputational risk. Most of the spend is committed before the market votes, so misses arrive late and expensive. The loop shifts cost to the margin; each cycle buys information as well as distribution, and "waste" converts into knowledge that compounds.

Algorithms enforce the distinction. They are automated gatekeepers that decide what reaches whom, optimizing not for pedigree or budgets but for signals of engagement, watch time, retention, shares, comments, return visits. They don't care whether the upload came from a studio or a teenager with a phone; they respond only to what keeps people in session.

And on the major feeds—YouTube, Instagram, TikTok —that bias is applied with total indifference to traditional markers of importance. What rises, over and over, is behavior: frequency you can keep, a voice that feels native, a pattern of small surprises that resets curiosity.

Power follows the structure. Pipelines centralize decisions through development, brand, and marketing as gatekeepers, using scarcity as their tool, while loops push power to the edge through operator autonomy, rapid iteration, and direct audience contact, using speed as their tool. Pipelines reward presentation, pedigree, packaging, and polish, while loops reward behavior—the consistent ability to win the next minute, the next return, the next share.

This is not an argument against craft but about when craft is proven—production logic perfects in private before exposing, while platform logic exposes early and perfects in public. The durable asset is no longer a single "hit"; it's a repeatable system—cadence you can keep, rules for format you can teach, rituals your audience recognizes, a backlog ranked by expected lift.

The failure modes diverge accordingly. Pipelines fail quietly then all at once—confidence holds until opening night and then the truth arrives—while loops fail loudly then improve, as the same visibility that punishes also instructs, and the operator who listens gets better in view of the crowd. One tries to script outcomes while the other discovers them by design, in public, and on repeat.

Legacy players saw the same signals, and assumed they could meet them with speed and budget. What came next was a series of expensive lessons on the folly of giving orders to loops.

Even as this pattern became clear, the establishment kept doubling down on production logic. The higher the stakes got, the more they insisted on applying old rules to new systems.

At Maker, we were getting calls from YouTube, which was throwing around serious money—$100 million across dozens of premium channels—and they wanted established talent. I sat in on conversations with reps for Ellen DeGeneres and Jennifer Lopez. The pitch was always the same: bring your TV sensibility to YouTube. We'll fund it, and you'll own the digital space.

But we could see the problem before any deals could close. When we explained YouTube's demands—weekly uploads, real-time audience engagement, platform-native content—Ellen's team seemed overwhelmed by the operational requirements. Even if they could pull it off, it would be a business obligation, not the authentic passion that drove successful YouTubers.

The fundamental mismatch was temporal. Television operates on seasonal cycles, develop, produce, market, air, repeat. YouTube operates on weekly or daily cycles, create, upload, engage, iterate. You can't just speed up television production; you have to think differently about what content is and how it functions.

YouTube viewers didn't want TV on YouTube. They wanted YouTube on YouTube. They wanted the immediacy, the direct access, and the continuous connection that defined the platform's native experience. The platform's appeal was proximity and intimacy, not the distant perfection of high-budget production.

This was a victory for the emergent creator. A major platform, with unlimited resources, had tried to steer its users toward more advertiser-friendly, legacy-style content—and the users simply refused. The platform adapted its strategy. Creators, once dismissed as amateur talent, were now undeniably the main event.

Meanwhile, Facebook was running its own expensive experiment in misunderstanding platform mechanics.

Around 2014, they approached us at Maker with what felt like a desperate play for video content. They wanted our YouTube creators' content on Facebook and Instagram, but the economics were deliberately murky. Instead of revenue sharing tied to actual consumption, they offered lump-sum payments that had no clear relationship to views, engagement, or any metric we could track.

It felt like buying video content by the pound. Facebook would write us a check for getting our creators to post natively on their platform, but we couldn't trace that payment back to how individual videos performed or which creators were actually driving value. It was the opposite of YouTube's transparent revenue split—there was no way to know if we were being overpaid, underpaid, or how to optimize for better results.

For creators, it was a black box. They'd cross-post to Facebook, see decent reach numbers, but have no idea if that translated to actual revenue or career growth. Facebook's model felt like they were paying us to legitimize their video ambitions while keeping the actual economics hidden.

Even Facebook's acquisition of Instagram in 2012 initially followed this pattern. Post-acquisition, they poured fuel on Instagram's growth, but their early attempts to monetize it relied on traditional advertising models rather than understanding the native influencer economy that was already emerging.

Every institutional attempt to impose traditional media logic onto emergent digital platforms failed. YouTube Originals, Facebook's video push, celebrity social strategies, all crashed against the same truth: authentic connection couldn't be manufactured from the top down, no matter how substantial the budget or how polished the production. The platforms consistently favored the organic over the orchestrated, the emergent over the engineered.

But while the establishment struggled to comprehend this new reality, dismissing it as amateur or unsustainable, creators themselves weren't waiting for institutional validation. They were building something entirely different.

What came later, TikTok's full emergence, proved the pattern once again. It borrowed from Vine's success but solved the monetization problem. Same addictive format, same raw authenticity, but with creator funds, brand partnerships, and revenue streams that Vine never developed. It succeeded because it built systems around what short-form creators were already doing, not because it tried to force them into traditional media models.

The more sophisticated the attempts to game these systems become, the more obvious they are to the audience they're trying to reach. The Monkees music factory hasn't gone anywhere. For a current example, look at the Korean boy and girl bands of this era: audition young, pretty talent, hire songwriters and production pros, train them to dance, dress them up, present them like *Teen Beat*. It's the same assembly line.

The algorithm can't tell the difference between real and fake engagement. It only measures clicks, shares, and watch time. Yet somehow, audiences still can. When authenticity becomes strategy, it stops being authentic. And platform users don't need an algorithm to spot the difference.

The biggest breakouts still emerge from genuine platform-native behavior. They aren't following a playbook because there isn't one yet. Their success comes from the same place as The Beatles': an authentic connection that no marketing department can reverse-engineer.

The industry kept trying to cast The Monkees while the platforms kept finding The Beatles.

2 BUILDING WITHOUT PERMISSION_

WHILE PLATFORMS and media companies repeatedly stumbled in their attempts to manufacture authentic creator success, something far more significant was taking shape in the margins. Creators who couldn't get past network gatekeepers, who watched their YouTube revenue vanish overnight when algorithms shifted, who saw brand deals evaporate without explanation—they stopped waiting for permission. They began building their own economic infrastructure, piece by piece, creating sustainable businesses that didn't depend on anyone else's rules.

Money always follows attention. And by 2011, the attention was undeniable—creators were pulling millions of views with bedroom setups and $200 cameras. This is where the Multi-Channel Network era began in earnest. The thesis was simple: individual creators had the audience, but they lacked the business infrastructure. We could be the bridge.

Companies like Maker Studios, Fullscreen, Machinima, AwesomenessTV, and StyleHaul emerged with a seemingly sensible thesis: creators had the audience, but they didn't know how to turn views into rent money. Platforms like YouTube offered distribution, but their creator support was basically non-existent, an email autoresponder and a revenue split that creators couldn't decipher. MCNs positioned themselves as the missing piece, offering brand deals, production resources, and someone to actually answer the phone when things broke. In exchange, they wanted 30 to 50 percent of everything a creator made. For struggling creators, it felt like a lifeline. For successful ones, it felt like robbery.

I started consulting for Blip in May 2012 and joined full-time that August. When Maker Studios acquired the company in August 2013, I moved into Maker's strategy and corporate development team. We weren't just aggregating talent; we were actively trying to build something that looked like the next Viacom or a new-era Disney. Think of it like a digital MTV, where each vertical—gaming, beauty, parenting, comedy—was run by creators who owned both the content and the conversation. Instead of executives in suits deciding what teens wanted to watch, we had actual teens making content for other teens.

Maker officially marketed 23 distinct verticals, but the broader ambition was clear: we wanted to industrialize digital creation without killing what made it special. The difference was, every creator was both the worker and the product. We built intuitive dashboards for creators, internal sales pipelines to attract brand dollars, and proprietary CMS and analytics tools designed to integrate creators into a larger monetization ecosystem. It was the closest anyone came to a coordinated, industrial-scale creator economy, a true factory floor for digital content.

The logic behind acquiring Blip was strategic. Maker, like other MCNs, was entirely dependent on YouTube's infrastructure, its algorithm, rules, and rev share terms. In 2013, what Google had done to Demand Media with the Panda search update was still fresh: an entire business model crushed because it didn't own its distribution. Blip brought a hedge: a cross-platform foundation Maker could control, along with talent and programming logic better suited to life beyond YouTube.

Blip wasn't just a platform; it represented an early experiment in creator-driven programming, valuing narrative and serialized storytelling over daily viral uploads. One of Blip's unique traits was its emphasis on serialized shows, with creators like Nostalgia Critic building seasons instead of chasing daily uploads. We pursued M&A, explored verticals like books and games, and began to think of ourselves not just as a network, but as a layer of infrastructure. Where Blip had tested intention at a smaller scale, Maker industrialized it.

And for a time, it genuinely seemed to work. Brands signed multi-million dollar deals with MCNs, eager to tap into digital audiences that traditional media couldn't reach. Disney, hardly a reckless acquirer, purchased Maker in early 2014 for $675 million, a staggering validation of the MCN model. The promise to creators was clear: MCNs would handle business, growth, and complexity, freeing them to focus on what they loved—creating.

One example of that in action was StampyLongNose. He was huge with kids but almost invisible outside the platform—Minecraft adventures narrated in real time, minimal editing, enormous loyalty. His audience watched religiously, rewatched constantly, and skewed so young they barely showed up in the demos that brands cared about.

When we partnered with him to produce *Wonder Quest* and *iWonder*, we weren't just "supporting a creator"; we were co-producing original IP. These were scripted, scored, fully animated series with educational tie-ins and recurring characters. We even did a book that sold over half a million copies. That was the MCN thesis working: take a native YouTube hit and help the creator make the leap from videos to a multi-platform brand.

And the conversations started to shift. Creators who'd started with webcams and bedroom setups were asking about studio space, teams, and how to compete with the bigger, more polished channels showing up on their homepages. The culture inside the network was changing. On the surface, it looked like everything we'd promised was coming true.

But beneath the surface, the cracks were already forming. I watched creators discover the hard way that scale doesn't always mean support. Maker's economics varied wildly across its creator tiers. Top creators, those driving major views and ad revenue, typically retained most of their existing AdSense income. Maker's share came from incremental monetization it helped generate: sponsorships, branded content, or platform partnerships. Mid-tier creators, who had some scale but lacked leverage, often gave up a more meaningful cut in exchange for limited support that didn't always materialize. And then there was

2 BUILDING WITHOUT PERMISSION

the longtail—thousands of small creators funneled into the Maker Gen program. They didn't give up much revenue, but they received even less in return: minimal communication, basic CMS access, and the distant hope of discovery or promotion.

I had regular conversations with the head of Maker Gen—not to defend the system, but because he cared deeply and was looking for help. He knew creators were frustrated. He heard it constantly: channels feeling invisible, misled, left behind. He wanted to fix it, but the problem wasn't attitude but architecture. We'd designed something that could scale, but not something that could support. The structure couldn't deliver what creators needed most: individual attention, tailored guidance, a sense that someone was actually in their corner. What was meant to be empowering started to feel transactional. And the more it grew, the worse it got.

Maker offered real value in areas like rights management and Content ID optimization, and its proprietary dashboards and packaging of YouTube data were useful for many creators. But as creators became more sophisticated, and more tools became natively accessible on YouTube, the perceived value of MCN support began to erode.

The collapse was swift and telling. Despite Disney's massive investment, Maker Studios was slowly suffocated by the very company that acquired it. Disney hadn't bought Maker to nurture its chaotic, creator-led ecosystem. It bought it for parts, for its rights-claiming expertise, brand deal execution, and a few pieces of useful infrastructure and personnel.

At first, there was confidence. Our internal champion was Disney CFO Jay Rasulo, widely expected to succeed Bob Iger as CEO. His support gave the deal momentum and offered Maker a degree of political protection. Ynon Kreiz, Maker's CEO and a Saban protégé, had previously sold Fox Kids Europe to Disney and knew how to navigate its internal gauntlet. For a while, that combination worked.

That protection evaporated quickly. Rasulo exited in summer 2015, and Kreiz followed at the end of the year. With both gone, Maker's fate fell into unsympathetic hands, executives who hadn't supported the deal from the start. By the time Jimmy Pitaro was overseeing our division, the acquisition had already become something he was known to have opposed.

What Maker had built was open, messy, and creator-first: something Disney was neither culturally prepared to support nor ever truly wanted. Disney was still Disney. It didn't see social video as a new operating model; it saw it as a promotional layer for its existing IP and talent. In that way, it followed the same logic as theAudience: traditional media using new platforms not to evolve, but to reassert control.

Fullscreen pivoted away from creator networks entirely. StyleHaul shut down operations. The promised "next Viacom" became a cautionary tale, not about digital creators, but about legacy media's inability to imagine a future it didn't control.

There wasn't a single reason MCNs broke. It was a pile-up. Founder ambition and VC greed pushed models past what the ecosystem could support. Acquirers brought their own ignorance and appetite for scale, assuming the machine could be industrialized. Platforms tightened rules and monetization with indifference to downstream fragility. The work itself was brutally labor-intensive, managing hundreds of creators with different sizes, rhythms, and needs. And all of it was happening too early, before the tools, norms, and economics had stabilized. Those failures didn't compete. They compounded.

Still, the MCN era left a clear legacy: it proved that creators were a powerful force, worth investing in on a massive scale. Its failure delivered an equally powerful lesson: creators didn't need legacy institutions to extract that value. They needed to be freed from them.

With the collapse of the MCNs and the clear failure of institutional video strategies, a new, simpler logic took hold that shifted the focus from content networks to individual reach: if creators were building massive, engaged audiences, then brands wanted in.

Marketers began allocating real budgets to social-first campaigns. The digital landscape exploded with specialized agencies and startups dedicated to tracking creator metrics, brokering brand deals, and building platforms for brand-creator collaboration. "Influencer" became a widely recognized category. Brand partnerships evolved rapidly from a fringe experiment into a legitimate, often incredibly lucrative, revenue stream for the top tier of digital talent.

This period introduced new tensions that still ripple through the creator economy today. Brands, accustomed to the rigid control of traditional advertising and wary of unpredictability, often demanded extensive oversight—scripting every word, dictating visuals, approving every post.

Creators, meanwhile, knew their audience's trust was their biggest asset—and the easiest thing to lose. I saw creators hesitate over sponsored posts—not because of any moral dilemma, but because a bad fit could ding their reputation or crater engagement. The money mattered, most were living deal-to-deal, but so did staying relevant and keeping the audience they'd fought to build.

Audiences, for their part, could spot a forced integration instantly and didn't hesitate to scroll past. That made every brand partnership a balancing act: maximize revenue without breaking the relationship that made it possible in the first place.

Influencer marketing succeeded wildly when creators retained their unique voice and their audience's trust remained intact. It flourished when the integration felt organic, like a genuine recommendation from a friend. It flopped spectacularly when brands tried to script everything, reducing creators to mere spokespeople—digital Monkees, packaged for virality by an industry still chasing a hit parade model.

The experiments that worked treated creators as programming partners, not promotional vehicles. At Blip, we'd developed *The Gauntlet*, a competition series cocreated with Rooster Teeth. Season one was fully sponsored by Geico, season two by Verizon—full-season, single-sponsor integrations that were virtually unheard-of for independent digital platforms. The format proved that web-native content could support television-level brand partnerships, but only when the relationship felt like genuine collaboration rather than hired promotion.

All the while, beneath the surface of MCN booms and

2 BUILDING WITHOUT PERMISSION

influencer marketing frenzies, something else was quietly happening: something far more durable. It was a shift born of necessity, a direct response to the limitations and frustrations of depending on platforms for survival.

Even by 2014, the warning signs were there. Creators would log in to find videos suddenly demonetized, views throttled by algorithm tweaks, or channels flagged for violations they didn't understand. Entire livelihoods could be destabilized without warning, and with no one to call. These weren't isolated incidents; they were early indications of a deeper vulnerability: creators had built their futures on systems they didn't control and barely understood.

Platforms like Patreon, Gumroad, and YouNow emerged—each offering creators new ways to bypass traditional gatekeepers and earn directly from their audiences. These weren't ad-dependent models driven purely by impressions; they were built on direct relationships between creators and their most engaged fans. For the first time, creators could directly build subscription tiers, offer premium content, sell digital products, or simply accept tips directly from their most loyal fans, bypassing the legacy gatekeepers and even the platforms' own ad systems.

This represented a fundamental shift in power dynamics. Instead of creating content that pleased algorithms and advertisers, creators could focus on serving their actual community—the people who cared enough to pay them directly.

This shift toward direct monetization wasn't happening in isolation. At Blip, where I'd worked in 2012–

2013, we weren't trying to manage creators on someone else's platform—we were building an alternative to YouTube entirely. We launched apps across Roku, Xbox, iOS, and Android, and closed seven-figure deals with partners like Fremantle, Ray William Johnson, and Grace Helbig to launch standalone web channels. The approach was different: treat creators as programmers, not uploaders. Build for serialized content, not viral clips. It was smaller than YouTube, but it operated on a different logic—one that prioritized curation over chaos.

Simultaneously, established platforms began integrating similar tools: Twitch introduced subscriptions and tips, YouTube added Super Chats and Channel Memberships, and even Instagram and TikTok flirted with creator funds and affiliate tools, acknowledging the growing power of direct fan support.

This was the real birth of the creator economy in its sustainable form—not just the ability to create content, but the infrastructure to monetize it directly, democratizing financial independence for creators with truly engaged audiences. It wasn't just about audience size anymore; it was about audience depth, about building relationships strong enough that people would pay to support the work.

And it didn't happen because a studio willed it into being, or because a tech giant designed it from scratch as a benevolent gift. It happened because creators, often locked out of traditional systems, frustrated by the limitations and volatility of ad-based models, and inspired by the possibilities of the internet, started solving problems for themselves. They figured out how to get paid without a greenlight. They learned how to build true community without a network's blessing. They innovated ways to merchandise their brands, crowdfund ambitious projects, organize tours and events, publish their own works, and grow their ventures—all without asking permission from traditional institutions, piece by piece.

Even as creators built their own infrastructure and forged new paths outside the confines of traditional media, they remained tethered to the logic and limitations of the platforms on which they depended. For all the autonomy that tools like Patreon, Gumroad, and Substack enabled, the broader creator economy was still deeply shaped by the architectural choices and incentive systems of the major platforms, particularly YouTube, TikTok, and Instagram.

These weren't neutral stages. Each platform came with its own embedded assumptions about what content should look like, how it should be distributed, and what behaviors should be rewarded. Instagram rewarded bright, curated, aspirational feeds. TikTok demanded speed, sound, and personality. Hook them in three seconds or lose them. YouTube favored long-form storytelling, but only if it delivered retention and met an ever-shifting matrix of monetization rules.

These weren't black-box mysteries. They were enforcement mechanisms—terms of service that went far beyond legal language, shaping culture and economics in real time. If you wanted visibility, you had to play by the rules. And the rules weren't posted; they were inferred, reverse-engineered, and endlessly gamed.

For creators, fluency in each platform's logic came at a

cost. As they gained audiences, they became more beholden to the systems they once sought to circumvent. Creative choices weren't just driven by audience desire, they were shaped by platform incentives. Titles were optimized. Thumbnails became battlegrounds. Pacing, editing, even subject matter bent toward what the algorithm rewarded.

I watched this shift up close, not just in the creators themselves, but in the teams built to support them. At Maker, we had dedicated strategists working with top-tier channels, helping them decode YouTube's ever-shifting signals and surface higher in recommendation feeds. Even our internal systems evolved to reflect the algorithm's preferences. It was like watching artists, managers, and marketers all become data analysts—constantly testing thumbnails, A/B-ing upload times, and fine-tuning content to chase what worked.

Some rules YouTube enforced selectively. Sponsorships baked straight into videos were everywhere, and YouTube seemed fine with it—until the FTC got involved. Overnight, the tone changed. "Paid promotion" tags appeared, #ad became standard, and creators were told compliance was their problem. The same platform that had looked the other way now wanted everything above board, leaving creators to retrofit transparency into a system that had thrived on the opposite.

This was the emerging paradox: creators had more independence than ever before, yet they were becoming more entangled in systems they didn't control. The old gatekeepers were fading, but new ones were taking their place—platforms whose preferences were enforced not by executives, but by code. You no longer needed permission to publish. But you still needed permission to be seen.

The real terms of service weren't in the fine print. They were baked into the infrastructure. And creators, whether they realized it or not, were always negotiating with the machine. The contract wasn't written in words, it was enforced in code.

This is the core, enduring lesson of the early 2010s creator economy, a truth that continues to resonate today: you cannot manufacture organic growth. You can accelerate it. You can amplify it. You can even guide it, through smart marketing and operational excellence. But you cannot fabricate it from the top down—not sustainably, not authentically.

The early efforts we've detailed—theAudience's attempts to industrialize celebrity influence, YouTube Originals' bid to turn the platform into traditional TV— were well-intentioned, backed by immense capital and experienced talent, but misaligned with the emergent digital reality. theAudience was trying to retrofit established celebrity into a new medium designed for two-way conversation. YouTube Originals was trying to retrofit the linear, episodic logic of television into a platform built for personal connection. In both cases, the logic of legacy media simply couldn't stretch far enough to meet the new physics of digital culture.

And that's why both efforts eventually faded—not with a bang but with a shrug. They failed because they assumed the enduring value lived in the format, the production quality, or the traditional intellectual property, the "what" of content. But the real, resilient, and scalable value lived in the relationship between creator and community, a relationship built on trust and shared identity, the "who" of connection. This was a value that defied top-down manufacturing.

Those early failures weren't wasted. They were necessary. They cleared space. They sent a signal to the entire industry. They showed the world what didn't work, and in doing so, gave creators the permission and the impetus to figure out what did work on their own terms, without waiting for institutional approval.

These failures also taught the platforms something important: don't chase Hollywood. Hollywood will eventually come to you. And it did. Eventually. But only once the new native class of creators had, through sheer force of organic will and emergent connection, built an audience too massive to ignore. That's when major brands started spending real money on social-first campaigns. That's when the Multi-Channel Networks formed. That's when platforms like YouTube built more robust creator tools. And independent platforms like Patreon and Substack emerged, offering direct monetization pathways. That's when Instagram launched Stories, directly copying a format proven successful by Snapchat, and Facebook started paying creators. That's when "influencer" became a widely recognized job title. That's when the creator economy transcended its niche origins and became a legitimate, multi-billion-dollar category.

But it all started with those early failures. With *The Monkees* moment, when the system tried desperately to simulate what hadn't yet emerged, and in doing so, showed

2 BUILDING WITHOUT PERMISSION 49

just how badly it misunderstood the very essence of the digital era.

Blip was the bridge that proved a bridge wasn't enough. Uploading TV didn't make TV native. It optimized for seasons and shows, not atomic clips and sessions; for packaging and pre-roll CPMs (cost per mille/thousand impressions), not retention and return. Without algorithmic distribution, durable identity, or native community, discovery stayed off-platform and gains didn't compound. It was bridge tech, and proof that platforms select behavior over pedigree.

Before feeds made video truly native, "online TV networks" tried to port a familiar playbook: pitch a concept, produce a season, premiere, promote, repeat. The unit of value was the show. Discovery depended on blogs, embeds, and PR. Monetization leaned on sponsorships negotiated off-platform. Success came in spikes—launch weeks, press hits, occasional homepage features—followed by long flats. The system didn't route viewers to the next thing automatically, and identity didn't persist in a way compounding attention could ride.

When feed platforms arrived with rails—algorithmic distribution tuned to retention, persistent identity that remembered you, native community that carried in-jokes forward, and payouts mapped to watch time—the unit of value shifted. Sessions beat seasons. Behavior beat presentation. Operators who kept attention inside the loop rose faster than concepts that only looked like television.

Those rails lead directly to the economics we turn to next: an attention market that behaves like a power law, not a middle class.

The creator economy has grown up. It has a name, playbooks, sophisticated infrastructure. Creator-led businesses now scale to unprecedented levels. The wild west of early YouTube has become an industry—professionalized, often corporatized, with its own conventions, investors, and power players.

But the pattern from the early 2010s is repeating. And if the last two decades of digital evolution have taught us anything, it's that transformative shifts rarely come from what's already visible or well-funded. They emerge at the edges, where constraints are few, experimentation runs unchecked, and nobody's waiting for permission.

Something's forming at the edge again.

You can feel it in the friction—algorithmic feeds against new formats; monolithic platforms against the people who populate them; manufactured spectacle against raw connection. It's in the burnout at the height of a boom. In the sameness of content tuned for the algorithmic treadmill. In creators quietly pivoting away from single-platform dependency, and in audiences drifting toward the niche. Kids skip the polished video for Minecraft worlds with friends or deep Discord channels built around specific obsessions. That tension isn't a flaw. It's the birthplace of the next wave of change.

Today, the creator economy is at another transitional moment, ambiguous, full of potential. Creators have more tools, reach, and leverage than ever. Yet platforms are shifting again. Algorithms evolve, often at the expense of discoverability and creator income. AI is commoditizing formats that once felt unique. Monetization is tightening,

2 BUILDING WITHOUT PERMISSION 51

squeezing the middle tier, the backbone of community-driven media, into a fight for sustainability.

At the same time, new openings are emerging. Decentralized platforms promise ownership and direct connection. Syndication models let creators distribute across ecosystems, breaking dependency on any one feed. Niche communities prove that depth can matter more than scale. The smartest creators aren't just building audiences; they're building sustainable ventures.

The tension is familiar: organic emergence vs. centralized industrialization. Bottom-up culture vs. top-down control. Disposable labor vs. independent entrepreneurs, and sometimes founders of entirely new media paradigms.

It feels like 2009 again. Or 2014. A moment of uncertainty, the quiet hum before the next phase clicks into place. What comes next may not look like YouTube. It may not be a single platform at all. But the pattern is the same: institutions scrambling to catch up to a shift that already happened, users migrating faster than strategy, creators once again building what the platforms failed to deliver.

In the next chapter, we'll look at the economics underpinning this new reality—why virality doesn't guarantee income, how visibility can mask fragility, and how the myth of the creator middle class props up false promises.

3 THE MYTH OF THE CREATOR MIDDLE CLASS_

We talk about the creator economy as if it's a marketplace. In theory, that implies a kind of bell curve: a few stars, a few strugglers, and a large, stable middle making a living doing what they love.

But that middle? It doesn't exist.

The creator economy is a power law, not a middle-class economy. The vast majority of creators earn little to nothing. A small percentage earn livable incomes. And an even smaller slice take home the kind of revenue that justifies teams, infrastructure, or true financial independence—not a failure of hustle but a feature of the platforms themselves.

The prevailing narrative of the creator economy paints an attractive picture of opportunity. It suggests a new kind of digital meritocracy, a place where raw talent, passion, and consistent effort are rewarded, leading to a sprawling middle class of independent artists, writers, musicians, and video makers. We're told the internet flattened the playing field, allowing anyone with a phone and an idea to build a sustainable living, free from the gatekeepers of old media. It's a comforting story, one that fuels millions of dreams and attracts countless aspirants.

But what if this widely accepted truth is, in fact, an illusion? What if the "creator middle class" is less a burgeoning reality and more a mirage? And what if our understanding of this economy is muddied by the conflation of two distinct roles: the creator and the influencer?

Understanding why the middle class remains a myth requires examining how platforms shape creator behavior at the most basic level. The economics are just one part of the story—the other is how the very structure of these platforms turns individual creators into components of a larger machine.

To understand the creator economy's true dynamics, we must first unbundle these often-interchanged terms. While both operate on social platforms and command audience attention, their primary motivations, metrics of success, and business models can differ significantly.

A creator is focused on producing original content, often driven by a passion for their craft: an artist, a musician, a writer, a detailed video essayist, a niche educator. Their success is rooted in the quality and uniqueness of their output and their ability to build a loyal audience around their work. Their ideal revenue streams might include direct payments from fans, selling merchandise, or licensing their original IP. Their primary goal is often to sustain their creative practice.

An influencer, on the other hand, is focused on building and leveraging a large, engaged audience for the purpose of brand partnerships and promotions. Their "content" often revolves around their lifestyle, opinions, or product endorsements. Their success is measured less by original artistic output and more by reach, engagement rates, and their ability to drive consumer behavior for brands. Their primary goal is often to monetize their audience's attention through sponsorships.

The influencer optimizes for the audience. The creator often begins by optimizing for the self. One reverse-engineers success; the other chases something more like voice or vision.

While the lines can blur—a creator might do brand deals, an influencer might make original content—the underlying intent often dictates their strategies and, crucially, their vulnerability to the system's pressures. Many creators are forced to become influencers to survive, sacrificing their original vision for brand visibility. The myth of the middle class conflates the influencer's often high-visibility, brand-dependent income with the creator's struggle for sustainable patronage.

While rare, there are platforms where something resembling a middle class has emerged, at least in pockets. Twitch is the clearest example.

Unlike the algorithm-driven feeds of TikTok or Instagram, Twitch is built on real-time interaction and fan-supported monetization. Streamers don't rely on being surfaced by a recommendation engine. They build habits. Viewers show up at the same time each day or week. They subscribe not just to consume content, but to be seen—to signal belonging, to chat with the creator, to get a badge next to their name. They're not chasing trends; they're building relationships.

And in this environment, something remarkable happens: creators with modest audience sizes can make a living. A streamer averaging 1,000 to 5,000 concurrent viewers might not even hit the radar on YouTube or Instagram. But on Twitch, that size is often enough to generate reliable monthly income through subscriptions, donations, and direct support—not superstardom but sustainability.

The dynamic is different. These creators aren't optimizing for the algorithm. They're not burning out trying to please sponsors. They're cultivating a deeply engaged niche, often in specific categories like gaming, commentary, music, or "Just Chatting." Many streamers know their top supporters by name. Community becomes both the content and the business model.

Of course, Twitch has its own challenges: long hours, harassment, platform dependency, the pressure to always be live. But the key distinction is this—income on Twitch is less tied to virality and more tied to ritual. Viewers don't drop in because the algorithm pushed a clip. They come back because it feels like home.

That's what a creator middle class might actually look like: not mass reach, but consistent connection. Not the pursuit of infinite scale, but the cultivation of depth—not the dominant model, but proof that a different one is possible.

The true economic landscape of the creator economy isn't shaped like a pyramid with a broad, flourishing middle, nor a gentle hill where most participants cluster around an average. Instead, it's a narrow, towering spire. In a power law, a very small number of participants achieve massive success, while the vast majority exist in relative obscurity, often earning little to nothing.

This isn't a new phenomenon but a recurring pattern that pervades professions offering high psychic reward—fields where the non-monetary benefits are immense, like fame, recognition, creative fulfillment, or simply the thrill of participation. Think about the entertainment industry: for every Hollywood A-lister or stadium-filling musician, there are thousands of incredibly talented actors waiting tables and musicians playing small clubs. The world of professional sports follows this pattern, with a few multi-million-dollar athletes and legions of equally dedicated but less compensated competitors. The allure of the top tier, the sheer desire to participate in a dream industry, creates an immense funnel of talent. The creator economy mirrors this, but with an even more pronounced effect due to its virtually non-existent barrier to entry.

This reality challenges the core tenet of a pure meritocracy, where hard work and talent are supposed to guarantee reward. In the creator economy, talent and effort are necessary, but almost never sufficient on their own. Millions of talented, dedicated creators upload content daily, often for years, without ever breaking through. The system is designed not for broad distribution of wealth, but for the exponential concentration of attention and, by extension, revenue.

We witnessed this dynamic firsthand at Maker Studios. At our peak, the Maker network boasted some 80,000 creators, a staggering number that spoke to the immense desire to participate in this new media landscape. Yet, when we looked at the economics, the power law was starkly evident. Of those

80,000 creators, perhaps only 2,000, a mere 2.5 percent, were making what could be called a living wage from their online efforts. From that 2,000, a much smaller group of around 200 made what we considered a truly newsworthy living. And it was creators like Shay Carl, CaptainSparklez, EvanTube, PewDiePie, and StampyLongNose who received the vast majority of our resources, our dedicated support teams, and our most lucrative brand deals. The concentration was even more extreme at the very pinnacle: these household names were responsible for 80 percent of Maker Studios' total revenue. Markiplier wasn't in that top tier initially, but grew into it, eventually becoming part of Revelmode alongside PewDiePie, JackSepticEye, and others until it shut down in February 2017. For the tens of thousands below them, the promise of a "creator career" remained largely unfulfilled.

Programs didn't flatten the curve; they often mapped to it.

TikTok's Creator Fund turned out to be a fixed pool divided among a growing set of creators—headline support with shrinking slices.

Partner rev-share systems (the classic "we pay when ads run" logic) distribute dollars in proportion to attention, not effort: so they naturally concentrate earnings where attention already pools. Even healthy absolute growth can mask widening relative inequality.

Direct-pay tools (tipping, subs, memberships) work best where ritual is strong and identity is clear; they create pockets of sustainability, not a platform-wide middle. Twitch showed how habit can fund a tier of working creators, but the success condition isn't "more creators," it's "more ritual." In other words: mechanics don't make a middle; behavior does.

This asymmetry of the power law, combined with the inherent unpredictability of viral success, creates a psychological paradox for creators. Even the very successful ones rarely know why they became successful. There's an enduring mystery to their breakthrough, a sense of "Why me?" rather than "I followed the perfect formula." This lack of clear causation can be both exhilarating and deeply unsettling.

Because the "why" remains elusive, creators naturally become intensely tied to the things they can control: their specific content format, their rigorous posting schedule, their distinctive style, even their precise editing techniques. They believe, often subconsciously, that their specific inputs are the magical ingredients that generated their past success. This leads to an understandable but often self-defeating reluctance to delegate tasks, to diversify content, or to adapt their approach. The idea of letting go—of a specific editing style, a particular niche, or even the painstaking manual labor of their craft—feels like abandoning the very thing that made them.

This mystery of why similar inputs produce wildly varying outputs is an emotional rollercoaster. A creator might spend weeks on a meticulously researched video, only to see it languish with a fraction of the views of a quickly assembled, more spontaneous piece. This emotional whiplash, this constant uncertainty, leads to burnout, self-doubt, and a desperate search for consistency where none is guaranteed. It's the psychological tax of a system built on unpredictable viral surges rather than stable audience growth.

The core reason this power law dominates, and why creators feel caught in this psychological trap, lies deep within the very engine of the modern internet: the platform algorithms. These aren't benevolent curators designed to uplift every artist and foster a middle class; they are complex, self-optimizing machines driven by a singular, overarching imperative: maximize overall user attention across the entire platform.

As a former colleague succinctly put it, "It's not your algorithm; it's their algorithm." And that "their" refers to the platform itself, whether you're a creator or an audience member. A platform like YouTube or TikTok isn't optimizing for your individual video's watch time, nor for your income, nor for your long-term creative fulfillment. It's optimizing for the aggregate watch time of all users, across all content, for as long as possible.

This focus on overall watch time has consequences. It favors content that is broadly appealing, highly clickable, easily digestible, and often follows established trends that have proven engagement. A creator who produces deeply niche, thoughtful, or experimental content might build a devoted, smaller audience, but they will struggle to gain algorithmic favor against influencers who excel at producing mass-appeal content or short, high-impact virals.

Take Johnny Harris, a creator known for meticulously researched, visually rich documentaries on geopolitics and history. His videos attract a highly engaged, intellectually curious audience, viewers who often watch to the end and share thoughtfully. But compared to prank channels or reaction influencers who churn out high-frequency, broadly appealing clips, his work doesn't always rise to the algorithm's surface. His audience might be loyal and attentive, but the algorithm reads that as one session. A reaction channel pulling millions of partial views registers as broader interest, even if that interest is fleeting.

This creates a subtle but pervasive feedback loop. Both creators and influencers, desperate for discoverability and a share of the platform's ad revenue, inevitably begin to optimize their content to align with algorithmic preferences. For the influencer, this might be a natural extension of their model—they are already optimizing for reach. But for the creator, this can be a creative struggle. They might shorten their videos, craft more sensational thumbnails, or chase trending topics even if these don't align with their authentic voice. This isn't a deliberate choice to abandon artistic integrity; it's a rational response to the system's incentives.

Algorithms struggle with context and nuance. Human taste is fluid, influenced by mood, company, time of day, and even the weather. An algorithm sees "watched *The Lord of the Rings*" and might recommend similar high-fantasy epics. It doesn't know you watched it with your fantasy-fanatic friend, but you prefer lighthearted comedies when you're alone.

On TikTok, the gap between behavior and intent becomes especially dangerous. A few seconds of watch time on a controversial clip can poison the algorithm for weeks. The platform sees every micro-interaction as signal, but it lacks context. It doesn't know if you were hate-watching, doom-scrolling, or just curious. That nuance, the ability to interpret behavior in a wider human frame, is what makes discovery feel right. TikTok's engine skips that step entirely.

And then there's the "black box" problem. As users, we rarely understand why we are being shown what we are. The recommendations arrive as cryptic pronouncements, without explanation or rationale. This opacity breeds frustration and distrust. When the system consistently gets it wrong, or when it reinforces our existing biases without introducing anything truly novel, we stop trusting it.

If there's a counterpoint, it's Twitch. Discovery there doesn't run through predictive engines. It runs through community. You find new creators because someone raids them after a stream, or because mods recommend them in chat. The signal comes from people you already trust, not from an abstract behavioral profile.

Even beyond direct platform monetization, the promise of external revenue streams, brand deals and sponsorships, often reinforces the power law, rather than ameliorating it. Brands, when looking for partners, are generally seeking vast reach and quantifiable impressions. They want influencers with large, active audiences, not necessarily creators with deeply loyal but smaller communities. This naturally funnels the vast majority of brand budgets towards the top tier of content providers.

Consider the early days of influencer marketing, where brands might engage a local foodie with 50,000 followers, hoping for a genuine, intimate connection with their niche audience. As the market matured, the pressure shifted. Brands wanted scale. Suddenly, that 50,000-follower creator struggled to get a meeting, while the influencers with millions of followers were fielding multiple offers a day.

The "influencer boom" has created new pathways for revenue, but it has also obscured the precariousness for many. For every mega-influencer earning millions, there are thousands of creators who land a handful of small, sporadic deals a year, barely covering their costs. These deals are often short-term, transactional, and provide no long-term stability. And as Chapter 1 highlighted, the audience can often detect a forced integration, leading to a loss of the very trust that made the creator valuable in the first place.

The "creator middle class" story persists because it's useful to almost everyone, except most creators. Platforms need limitless supply; the hope of sustainable income keeps uploads flowing and strengthens platform leverage at the top. A believable middle signals "fair odds," which lowers churn and quiets complaints about concentration. Investors like growth narratives powered by a broad, happy base. Agencies and tools sell playbooks, the more people who believe there's a repeatable path, the more demand for services that promise to unlock it. Media prefers hero arcs and how-to templates; nuance doesn't headline.

Brands also benefit. A perceived middle class implies an efficient long tail of "cost-effective" partners, which exerts price pressure on mid-tier creators and keeps CPM expectations contained.

Creators themselves sometimes keep the myth alive out of necessity. It's morale. It's recruiting collaborators. It's explaining to family why "this is working." It's telling an audience the ladder is climbable—because hope is part of the product.

None of this requires conspiracy. Incentives are enough. The myth is not a data claim; it's an onboarding narrative. It sustains participation long after the payout curve has told the truth.

The creator economy wasn't planned with a middle class in mind; it emerged. And because it emerged from a complex interplay of human desire, technological evolution, and powerful commercial incentives, it carries the inherent biases of those forces. It wasn't built with the intention of creating a sustainable middle class, but rather as an efficient mechanism for aggregating and monetizing attention on a massive scale.

This isn't to say creators or influencers don't earn money, or that breakthrough success isn't possible. It simply means that the distribution of that success is overwhelmingly uneven. The idea of a broad, thriving "creator middle class" is a comforting fiction, a widely held belief that masks a far more competitive and unequal reality.

This harsh reality of the power law creates enormous pressure on creators. Those struggling in the long tail don't just face financial challenges, they face an existential choice: adapt their content to what the algorithm rewards, or remain authentic but invisible. This pressure, multiplied across millions of creators, doesn't just affect individual careers. It shapes the very nature of content itself, pushing the entire ecosystem toward a kind of manufactured sameness that serves the platform's needs above all else.

Worse, the very notion of a middle class is used as

3 THE MYTH OF THE CREATOR MIDDLE CLASS

branding. Platforms tout creator funds, monetization programs, tipping features, as if these tools enable meaningful economic participation. But most of them are window dressing. They reward quantity, not quality. Participation, not ownership.

Nowhere is this more apparent than on TikTok, where the much-touted Creator Fund became a cautionary tale of platform incentives masquerading as creator support. The TikTok Creator Fund was launched with a promise: if you could capture attention, the platform would reward you for it.

Part of the problem was structural. The fund was fixed in size—a capped pool divided among a growing number of eligible creators. As more joined, everyone's share shrank. There was no floor, no transparency, and no way to build a stable income. Even creators who "won" the virality lottery found the prize to be worthless.

And yet the fund worked exactly as intended, for TikTok. It generated headlines about creator support. It kept the dream alive. It suggested a middle class was forming. But behind the scenes, it reinforced the same dynamics we've seen across every platform: high churn, opaque incentives, and an economic model that thrives on limitless supply and replaceable labor.

TikTok didn't need to make creators sustainable. It just needed them to believe sustainability was possible.

The creators who last, the ones who build actual careers, don't do it because the platforms supported them. They do it in spite of the platforms. They don't win by playing the algorithm's game a little better. They win by opting out of the game wherever they can.

They build parallel systems: email lists, merch drops, private communities, paid courses, direct brand licensing, even their own back-end CRMs. They create revenue streams the platform can't take away. And they build audiences that aren't just scrolling—they're opting in.

From the outside, these creators still look like individuals. But under the hood, they're often operating like companies. Sometimes with help: a partner, a part-time operator, a business-savvy sibling. Sometimes alone, MacGyvering systems together after midnight.

But the throughline is structure. Not polish. Not professionalism. Just repeatable, survivable operations.

That structure becomes leverage. And that leverage becomes longevity.

You won't find this in a YouTube tutorial or TikTok growth hack. But if you peel back the curtain on nearly every creator who's made it out of the long tail, you'll find the same pattern.

They didn't just post content. They built systems.

Let me show you what that looked like up close.

Before the term "creator economy" had any traction, I was already working with creators who'd built their own. No team. No budget. Just systems held together with duct tape, spreadsheets, and intuition.

At Maker, you could see the same pattern everywhere. Not one creator here or there—this was visible across the network. Creators weren't waiting for the business model to show up; they were hacking together the missing pieces of a business stack that didn't exist yet—duct-tape subscriptions on PayPal and Mailchimp years before Patreon, hand-run customer support for their own merch,

3 THE MYTH OF THE CREATOR MIDDLE CLASS

homegrown audience segmentation in Google Analytics so they could price brand deals with a little more precision.

They weren't just chasing views; they were compensating for a missing layer of infrastructure. The system didn't support them, so they built around it: tracking affiliate revenue from multiple vendors in a single spreadsheet, reconciling different payout structures by hand; designing their own thumbnails, running A/B tests, and manually logging performance long before YouTube offered meaningful tooling. From the outside it looked like hustle. From my vantage point, it was unpaid R&D for an industry that hadn't caught up yet.

It wasn't pretty, but it worked. What these creators lacked in polish, they made up for in operational creativity. And whether they knew it or not, they were building something that resembled real infrastructure: process, measurement, optimization. The raw stuff of a business.

Most weren't trying to scale. They were trying to survive. But survival required systems, and systems became leverage. Over time, that leverage compounded. The creators who lasted weren't always the most gifted on camera. They were the ones who treated every part of the operation, from upload to invoice, as their responsibility.

The platforms didn't reward that kind of work. No algorithm detected operational resilience. No trending tab elevated margin discipline or CRM fluency. But behind nearly every creator who made it out of the long tail was someone who figured out how to build structure in a system optimized for chaos.

They weren't content creators. They were operators in disguise.

At Maker, we saw firsthand what a structured creator business could look like at scale. The top 1 percent of our talent, those making real money, weren't flying solo. They had managers, production support, distribution deals, and in some cases, actual business units. And Maker itself provided scaffolding: a sales team to close brand deals, engineers to manage channel infrastructure, even physical studios to streamline output. For a handful of creators, we'd built a shadow studio system. Not because they were the most talented—but because we could attach infrastructure to their already proven reach. That's what scaled them further.

That infrastructure, combined with visibility, earned some of our creators access to premium opportunities like YouTube Red. We helped produce shows like *Scare PewDiePie* in collaboration with Skybound Entertainment —premium opportunities with actual production budgets that were only available to the platform's most valuable talent. This created another layer of separation between the top tier and everyone else.

The myth of the middle class persists because it's useful. It suggests that platforms are democratizing success. That access equals opportunity. That with enough effort, anyone can make it. But the truth is more complex. The creator economy is accessible, but it's not equitable. It's expansive, but not stable. And the systems in place are optimized for churn, not sustainability.

There's a better model. But to get there, we have to stop treating creators as content factories and start seeing them as businesses. Not every creator needs millions of followers. But every creator who wants to build something lasting needs structure.

The next wave of creator support won't come from tips or funds or stickers. It'll come from infrastructure: people, tools, strategies, and systems that help creators operate like companies, without losing what made them worth watching in the first place.

The middle class we want won't emerge from better algorithms. It'll emerge from better models. Think of Hank Green's education empire, or Rhett & Link's media studio, what looks like personality is often powered by process.

4 CREATORS AS MACHINES_

TRUE INDEPENDENCE EXISTED BEFORE PLATFORMS. Web developers in the late '90s built their own sites, owned their domains, controlled their content. Small audiences, but total ownership.

Then platforms arrived with a promise: democratize creation. Anyone could publish. No technical skills required. Massive reach.

Early creators thought they were reclaiming independence—digital punks rejecting the overproduced excess of mainstream media. They didn't realize they were trading ownership for reach, becoming the first unwitting employees of systems that would soon treat them as interchangeable machinery.

If the myth of the middle class is the lie creators are sold, the factory model is the system they're fed into.

The internet, we're told, democratized creativity. It gave a voice to millions, unleashing an unprecedented explosion of unique expression. Platforms, those digital town squares, loudly champion this diversity, celebrating breakout stars and viral sensations as testaments to their open, meritocratic systems. Yet, look closely at the most successful content on these platforms, and a curious paradox emerges: amidst the celebrated "creativity," there's a drive towards sameness.

This isn't an accident. Not a conspiracy in the smoke-filled-room sense, but a conspiracy of incentives. Like gravity, it doesn't need a plan to keep you on the ground. It's the inevitable outcome of what we might call the Platform Factory Model. These digital ecosystems, for all their veneer of spontaneous connection, operate with the precision and efficiency of a vast assembly line. Their ultimate product isn't original art or deep thought; it's user attention. And like any efficient factory, they optimize their inputs, the creators themselves, to churn out their desired output: maximum watch time, infinite scroll, and endless engagement.

As user-generated content evolved from novelty to industry, platforms perfected different pressures. What emerged wasn't a conspiracy but a pattern—each innovation training creators toward a new kind of optimization, each shift narrowing the path to success.

YouTube taught creators to read dashboards. I saw the earliest signs of this with EvanTube. What started as a kid unboxing toys in 2011 quickly evolved into something else entirely. By 2014, it was a highly polished operation—custom intros, licensed music, regular upload schedules, brand deals from Hasbro, WWE, and others. His sister joined the channel. Their dad ran the business. It was professionalized family content, engineered for scale.

Years later, Ryan's World would follow the same path—

4 CREATORS AS MACHINES 73

transforming kid-driven curiosity into a global licensing empire worth hundreds of millions. But the blueprint was already there, carved into YouTube's Creator Studio dashboard.

At Maker, I watched this transition happen in real time. Top creators weren't just uploading—they were being coached. Talent managers prepped them for brand-facing moments, translating creator performance into advertiser language. Internal pitch decks broke down audience demographics, retention curves, and brand alignment. The language shifted from "I love doing this" to "my audience delivers."

The dashboard didn't just inform. It trained.

Take YouTube's Creator Studio. It doesn't just show view counts—it breaks down where viewers drop off, second by second. A creator sees their philosophical 10-minute video essay has a 40 percent retention rate, while their quick reaction video hits 70 percent. The dashboard doesn't explain that the essay might have deeper impact or build stronger community. It simply presents the stark numerical comparison.

Over time, creators learn to chase the 70 percent. What looked like play became performance. Kid became brand. The data didn't lie—it just didn't tell the whole truth.

YouTube didn't reward originality so much as repeatability. And repeatable behavior could be measured, coached, and scaled.

Then TikTok arrived, and velocity became the new religion.

In 2018, TikTok launched in the U.S. with a feed design that changed everything. No subscriber tab. No friend circle. No expectation that a viewer ever builds a lasting relationship with a creator. Every swipe is a clean slate. Hook in three seconds or die.

By 2020, the pressure was visible. When Among Us exploded on streaming platforms, Marcus Bromander—one-third of the game's three-person development team—found himself trapped in an algorithmic sprint. The game had been out for two years with modest success. Then TikTok's recommender caught it. Overnight, everyone was streaming Among Us.

Bromander streamed for 42 days straight. Not by choice, but by necessity. If you weren't live when the trend peaked, you disappeared. In a 2021 interview he simply said: "We were three people. I played it in my sleep. It broke us."

This wasn't burnout from hard work. It was burnout from velocity—the understanding that the algorithm's attention span was shorter than your ability to rest. TikTok didn't just reward frequency. It demanded it. Post daily or become invisible. Chase the trend or watch someone else take your spot.

What Bromander lived through wasn't just the pressure to post; it was what happens when the factory moves inside the app.

TikTok doesn't just optimize content; it industrializes feedback in real time. YouTube trained creators to log in the next day and read a dashboard. TikTok makes the dashboard the experience. Views, likes, completion rate, rewatch percentage—every signal is instant, public, and directly wired to the next spin of the For You Page.

The result is a fully reactive production line. A sound

takes off at 9 a.m., and by noon the feed is flooded with variations. A micro-expression or camera angle spikes retention for one creator, and within hours it's canon across a million derivative clips. Creators post three, four, five times a day, A/B-testing hooks the way assembly workers once tweaked conveyor speeds. The morning batch teaches the afternoon batch; the loop never sleeps.

There are no creative directors, no notes sessions, no brand-safety memos. Just inputs and outputs, reward and punishment, all enforced by the algorithm in milliseconds. Content becomes raw material, performance becomes code, and the platform itself is the foreman—silent, relentless, perfectly scalable.

This is the Platform Factory Model with the safety rails removed. The machine no longer sits beside the creator. It lives inside the feed, inside the finger that refreshes one more time, inside every decision about what to post next. Once that loop closes, "creative freedom" starts to feel like a quaint phrase from an earlier operating manual.

TikTok added something else: identity reset. On YouTube, subscribers create continuity. On Instagram, followers build equity. On TikTok, every swipe is Groundhog Day. One viral video doesn't ladder to the next. The system doesn't care who made the last hit—it cares what performs now.

That design creates astonishing reach. Unknown creators can rack up millions of views overnight. But the reach is rarely stable and almost never compounding, because the product isn't built to grow creator equity. It's built to maximize viewer time spent. One hit resets the clock. That's why even many of TikTok's top creators eventually migrate elsewhere—to YouTube, to podcasts, to Discord—in search of something sustainable. TikTok may be the best discovery engine ever built. It's a terrible home.

For most creators, the churn is brutal. They burn through formats, trends, even pieces of their own identity trying to stay visible. The most successful don't just post—they study the feed like engineers. They A/B-test hooks, analyze drop-off rates, reverse-engineer trending audio patterns. They treat the algorithm not as a mystery but as a client to be served. And that client only cares about one thing: what will keep the next swipe from being the last.

This is the endpoint of optimization: a platform where every variable can be tuned, every outcome gamed, and every act of creation risks becoming just another input in a perfectly calibrated loop. If earlier platforms nudged creators toward sameness, TikTok hardwires it.

By 2020, the convergence was complete. YouTube launched Shorts. Instagram launched Reels. Every major platform copied TikTok's format, importing its velocity pressure while maintaining their own flavors of control. The result is a creator economy where the same factory logic operates everywhere, just with different branding.

Instagram added its own twist. Reels grafted TikTok's short-form treadmill onto a platform already defined by aesthetic perfection. The result wasn't just speed—it was uniformity at scale.

The "get ready with me" format became the template. Lighting flawless. Product application precise. Narrative concise, building to a dramatic reveal. Creators quickly noticed: certain camera angles drove higher engagement. Specific emotional beats kept viewers watching. The format wasn't just popular—it was algorithmically preferred.

Deviate from the template, and your reach collapsed. Post a casual selfie, an off-brand moment, an experimental angle? Reach drops 70 percent. The Instagram algorithm, fine-tuned for Reels, didn't just favor certain content. It punished variance.

Beauty didn't vary. It templated. The aesthetic pressure wasn't new—Instagram had always rewarded visual polish. But Reels accelerated it, marrying TikTok's velocity to Instagram's perfectionism. The result: thousands of creators producing nearly identical content, differentiated only by face and product, not by vision.

Instagram didn't reward making things. It rewarded being someone. Aesthetic was the achievement. The template was the product. GRWM wasn't about teaching technique—it was about performing personality, aspirational and brand-safe and endlessly repeatable. You didn't need skill. You needed a look.

While platforms competed on features—velocity, aesthetics, algorithmic feeds—a different kind of pressure evolved quietly in the background. Policy. Terms of service. The clickwrap contract creators agreed to but rarely read.

This pressure was different. YouTube's dashboard arrived as innovation. TikTok's feed launched as revolution. Instagram's aesthetic demands came as competitive response. But the clickwrap contract? It was there from the beginning, tightening slowly, like a python, until escape became impossible.

LazarBeam, 20 million subscribers, got demonetized. No warning. No negotiation. No meaningful appeal. Too big to delete outright—that would make headlines. But not too big to punish. The platform still controlled the money valve. The clickwrap contract he signed in 2009 made it legal.

Now consider the smaller creator. A channel with 100,000 subscribers, five years of daily uploads, thousands of hours of content. Flagged for a linked dormant account with old strikes. Deleted overnight. No warning. No human review. The appeal process, automated. The result, final. Chats. Mods. Five years of work. Gone.

Small or large, the contract was the same. Before uploading a single video, creators signed away their IP rights, their due process, their right to sue, their negotiating power. The terms of service granted platforms near-total discretion. Violations could be interpreted broadly. Enforcement, once delegated to algorithms, became a black box.

You didn't own your channel. You leased it. And the lease could be revoked without explanation.

In 2005, YouTube's moderation was manual. Flagged videos went to human reviewers. Decisions took days. Creators could appeal, explain, negotiate. By 2010, Content ID automated copyright claims. By 2015, algorithmic strikes replaced human review for most violations. By 2024, deletion could be instant.

The first three innovations—data dashboards, velocity feeds, aesthetic conformity—arrived as revolutions. Sudden. Visible. Celebrated. The fourth was there from the beginning, slowly tightening its grip. Manual review became Content ID. Content ID became algorithmic strikes. Algorithmic strikes became instant deletion. Each tightening felt reasonable in isolation. Together, they built a cage.

The psychological toll is immense. When the dashboard moves inside the feed, the pressure shifts from "post more" to "be more"—more available, more responsive, more whatever just worked. On the fastest platforms, you feel it in your body: stopping even briefly feels like disappearing. Always on. Afraid the next miss makes you disappear. Surveys of creators keep landing in the same place: burnout isn't an outlier, it's the default. The line between "who I am" and "what I create for the algorithm" blurs, leading to a sense of self-commodification where identity becomes inextricable from output.

When the logic of the platform becomes the logic of the creator, something gets lost. Risk, experimentation, voice, timing. The ability to step back. The capacity to stop. Creativity narrows to what performs.

Creators churn out videos not because they have something to say but because the schedule demands it, because the metrics indicate that a particular format is "performing." The internal conflict between selling out and merely surviving becomes a daily battle. And layered on top is the unique pressure of parasocial relationships—the one-sided intimacy audiences feel with creators. Fans who believe they "know" you demand constant engagement, personal updates, adherence to specific content types. It's emotional labor that compounds the algorithmic pressure, blurring the boundaries between personal and professional life, trapping the creator in a perpetual state of "being on" for both the algorithm and the audience it serves.

This factory model is particularly taxing for genuine creators who value originality and depth. For influencers, whose core value proposition is tied to brand alignment and trend participation, the pressure to conform might feel less disruptive. But for the artist, the educator, the storyteller, being forced into algorithmic molds turns creative practice into an optimization problem with no solution, only a treadmill that speeds up the longer you stay on it.

The problem isn't effort. It's environment. If you design a system to produce interchangeable outputs, it will eventually train interchangeable inputs. And when creators become fungible, it doesn't just hurt them—it devalues the whole ecosystem.

The paradox intensifies: platforms preach individuality and empower the "everyday person" to become a star, yet their core mechanisms push those individuals towards uniformity. This creates a deeply imbalanced ecosystem where individual creative authenticity is celebrated in rhetoric but commodified in practice. It leaves millions of aspiring creators trapped in a cycle of endless production, striving for a middle class that the very system they contribute to is structurally incapable of producing.

The idea of content creators as "machines," or the pressure for conformity within a "factory" system, isn't entirely new. Traditional media also had its own versions of optimization and control. Hollywood studios, for decades, perfected the assembly-line production of genre films, often signing actors to long-term contracts that dictated their image and roles. Network television became masters of the "sitcom formula" or the "procedural drama template," driven by ratings and advertiser demands that mirrored today's "watch time" imperative. Pop music labels consistently pushed artists towards commercially viable sounds and manufactured images, often sacrificing artistic integrity for radio play.

However, the digital "Platform Factory" introduces new pressures that amplify these old patterns.

Speed and Volume: Traditional media had production cycles, often measured in months or years. Creators in the platform factory are expected to be "always on," churning out content daily or weekly, a pace that makes deep, reflective creative work incredibly challenging.

Direct and Instant Feedback: Traditional media relied on delayed Nielsen ratings or box office numbers. Digital dashboards provide real-time, granular data on every single piece of content, intensifying the optimization pressure in ways never before possible. Creators know within hours if their content is "working" or not, leading to immediate, often panicked, adjustments.

Individual Pressure: In traditional media, studios or networks absorbed creative and financial failures; there was a buffer. Now, individual creators bear the full psychological and financial burden of their output. They are the factory, the product, and the marketing department all at once.

Algorithmic Black Box: Traditional media had human gatekeepers whose decisions, though biased, could at least be understood, appealed to, or sometimes reasoned with. The algorithm's judgments are often opaque, its criteria inscrutable, leaving creators battling an invisible, unfeeling force whose logic can seem arbitrary.

Granularity changed the game. Old factories optimized by season and quarter; digital platforms optimize by second and session. When feedback resolves at frame-level and payouts resolve at watch-time-level, the path of least resistance narrows to what survives the first few seconds. Formats don't just repeat—they converge. Same song, double speed.

It's an older pattern, certainly, this drive for efficiency and mass appeal. But in the digital age, it has been amplified and accelerated to a dizzying, often dehumanizing, degree, creating a new set of challenges for the individuals who pour their lives into becoming cogs in the machine.

This obsession with total watch time changes everything. The algorithm doesn't reward brilliance—it rewards behavior. It favors what's clickable, repeatable, safe. What works for everyone.

Early creators thought they were building businesses. They were building inventory. They thought they were independent. They were the first unwitting employees.

What began as a revolution starts to feel like a loop. Creators burn out. Audiences tune out. The system eats itself.

And in the end, it looks a lot like the thing it set out to replace. Television.

PART 2
POWER_

The creator economy was meant to share the spoils. Attention was supposed to come with power. Gatekeepers would fall, and the field would level. Anyone with talent and drive could build an audience, steer their own fate, and own the value they made.

That's not what happened.

Creators worked harder for less predictable returns while platforms kept most of the value and creators carried most of the risk. Ownership was an illusion—severed in an instant by a tweak to the feed.

AI doesn't displace creators first. It displaces the paid work around them. Editing, packaging, and audience ops get automated because the tools are cheaper. Budgets tighten, platforms keep more of the margin, and creators remain the irreplaceable input—the last human layer left.

From there, these chapters trace how power actually flows: YouTube's evolution from video-sharing site to television network; the gap between "owning" an audience and actually controlling one; the collapse of discovery into a crisis of connection; and how the sharpest creators build parallel infrastructure—identity, syndication, membership—to drive return and restore balance.

This isn't just business models or platform politics. It's about agency in a system built for dependence, the gap between visibility and actual viability, and what it takes to build something sustainable when the rules can change overnight.

The creator economy was sold as independence. The reality is dependence—and it's more fragile than anyone wanted to admit.

Power follows attention, and when platforms hold both, creators are left holding the bag.

5 WHEN YOUTUBE BECOMES TV_

YOUTUBE WASN'T BUILT to be television. That was the point.

It was raw, chaotic, unpredictable—everything TV wasn't. There were no gatekeepers. No formats. No time slots. It was the domain of vlogs, jump cuts, overshares, and "what's up guys" intros. For a generation raised on programming they didn't control, YouTube was theirs.

And then it started to look a lot like television.

The prevailing image of YouTube still carries echoes of its early days: raw, unpolished videos filmed in bedrooms, spontaneous vlogs, and niche passions finding unexpected audiences. Yet, if you look at the most dominant channels today, particularly in unscripted video, a different reality emerges. The humble bedroom has been replaced by sprawling soundstages, casual vlogs by carefully planned spectacles, and amateur creators by multi-million-dollar production enterprises. YouTube, in its relentless pursuit of attention, has morphed into something eerily familiar: it has become the new television.

No one embodies this transformation more than MrBeast. Jimmy Donaldson began like many others: a kid filming videos in his backyard. But his ambition quickly outstripped the conventional YouTube playbook. His content isn't just viral but an escalating series of grand challenges and philanthropic stunts: burying himself alive for 50 hours, buying everything in a store, giving away millions of dollars, or recreating the set of *Squid Game* with real contestants and a $456,000 prize. This isn't lo-fi authenticity but creator-led unscripted spectacle, operating at a scale that rivals, and often surpasses, traditional broadcast productions.

MrBeast's journey is a masterclass in understanding and leveraging the Platform Factory Model from Chapter 4. He grasped that YouTube's algorithms, obsessed with maximizing watch time, would reward content that consistently delivered peak engagement to the broadest possible audience. He didn't just make videos but engineered experiences designed to be irresistible to the widest demographic. The point of spending millions isn't excess—it's to feed the algorithm a spectacle it can't ignore.

To be clear: this isn't about quality. MrBeast and creators like him are brilliant at what they do. They've cracked the code. But the code itself is starting to feel familiar, and not in a good way. When everyone's chasing retention curves and global reach, the result starts to flatten. The tone changes. The medium hardens into a genre.

This pattern isn't unique to YouTube—it's a recurring cycle across creative industries. The music industry followed the same arc: in the 1970s, production was controlled by labels with expensive studio infrastructure, but by the early 2000s, digital tools like Pro Tools and GarageBand brought studio-quality recording to personal computers, while platforms like MySpace and SoundCloud enabled direct distribution. The transformation followed a predictable sequence: high barriers to entry give way to toolchain disruption, which enables platform shifts, which create new power structures. What used to require a village now requires a laptop—a phenomenon sometimes called "toolchain compression." YouTube's evolution from bedroom vlogs to broadcast-scale productions represents the latest iteration of this pattern, where the democratizing tools that broke down barriers eventually enable a new generation of creators to rebuild those same barriers at scale.

MrBeast's success isn't just about big ideas but about the sophisticated operation behind them. His early videos were simple: counting to 100,000. But his insight was clear: even mundane tasks could be compelling if presented with extreme dedication and framed for maximum curiosity. As he grew, so did his budgets and his team. What began as a solo endeavor evolved into a thriving enterprise with dozens of employees, dedicated production crews, editors, sound designers, and business strategists. This isn't one person with a camera but a media company built around a single personality.

The money behind these spectacles is enormous, far beyond what typical YouTube ad revenue could sustain. MrBeast's budgets—often millions per video—come from a diverse ecosystem: lucrative brand deals integrated seamlessly into his stunts, substantial merchandise sales, and significant investments from platform funds or private investors eager to back a proven attention-generating machine. These are not just content pieces but tentpole events, carefully planned for viral distribution and sustained engagement.

This new scale redefines "authenticity" on YouTube. While MrBeast's persona is genuine in its relentless ambition and passion for spectacle and generosity, it's a different kind of authenticity than the relatable rawness of early YouTube. Early creators were authentic because they were often unfiltered reflections of everyday life. MrBeast's authenticity lies in his genuine commitment to the outlandish, his pursuit of ever-larger, more impactful stunts. His is the authenticity of relentless ambition.

MrBeast represents something new: a creator who has achieved such scale that the traditional creator/influencer distinction becomes meaningless. He creates genuinely original content, elaborate challenges and philanthropic spectacles that define aspirational entertainment, but he does so within a fully industrialized system optimized for maximum algorithmic impact. He's not an influencer masquerading as a creator, or a creator who sold out. He's what happens when authentic creative vision successfully scales within platform logic.

However, this pursuit of hyper-scale forces creators to abandon the niche, the raw, or the deeply personal content that once defined the platform. To appeal to hundreds of millions, you must shed specificities that might alienate a broad audience. The content becomes optimized for universal understanding and maximal impact, pushing toward genres like challenges, philanthropic gestures, or massive-scale experiments that transcend cultural or demographic boundaries. The nuanced, introspective vlog often gives way to the high-concept stunt.

The rise of creators like MrBeast isn't an isolated anomaly but part of a broader pattern of content scaling that has seen diverse personalities and studios emerge as the new broadcast networks. These are figures and entities that mastered the platform's core directive, capturing and holding mass attention, often long before traditional media fully grasped the shift.

Jake and Logan Paul became early, often controversial, pioneers of this new age of digital spectacle. Their early strategies revolved around understanding virality, creating planned events, and engineering controversies that generated massive attention. While their content sometimes bordered on the outrageous and sparked widespread debate, they demonstrated a raw understanding of how to leverage platform algorithms for maximum reach.

Smosh, one of YouTube's oldest and most iconic channels, launched in 2005. Starting as simple lip-sync videos and evolving into sketch comedy, Smosh showcased the early potential of digital-native talent. Their journey—marked by immense popularity, acquisition by a Multi-Channel Network (Defy Media), and later a buy-back by the original founders—tells a story of creative control vs. corporate scale. Even under larger corporate umbrellas, Smosh adapted by expanding into multiple channels (Smosh Games, Smosh Pit) and bringing in an ensemble cast, demonstrating a continuous drive for diversified, scalable content. Their evolution from two friends making jokes to a mini-media conglomerate highlights the pressures to professionalize and expand just to stay relevant.

Dude Perfect represents the polished, high-production, family-friendly side of scaled spectacle. Their brand is built around incredible trick shots, elaborate challenges, and relatable camaraderie. They consistently deliver visually impressive, broadly appealing entertainment that resonates with a massive demographic. Their videos often involve complex setups, specialized equipment, and a large team, showcasing how consistent, high-quality, and highly repeatable formats can build an empire. They are entertainment technologists as much as performers, perfecting the art of repeatable, engaging spectacle.

By the time Hot Ones booked Gordon Ramsay in 2019, it had already cemented its place as a cultural phenomenon. But what made it remarkable wasn't just the caliber of its guests but the fact that it never left. Hot Ones didn't start on cable and migrate to YouTube. It wasn't optioned by a network, reformatted for streaming, or distributed through traditional syndication channels. It was, and remains, a show born of YouTube, built for YouTube, and perfected on YouTube. It became television without ever bothering to ask TV's permission.

Created in 2015 by Chris Schonberger and hosted by Sean Evans, Hot Ones began as a quirky food-interview hybrid under Complex Networks' food vertical First We Feast. The premise was simple: interview celebrities while they eat progressively hotter chicken wings. But that simplicity was deceptive. The format was ingenious, repeatable, memeable, and modular. It played like a talk show, but it moved like the internet: fast, reactive, and built for clipping. Evans' research-intensive interview style gave it legitimacy, while the hot wings gave it a gimmick that couldn't be replicated by traditional press junkets or studio talk shows.

Over time, Hot Ones layered on rituals: the Scoville heat scale graphic, the glass of milk, the recurring catchphrases ("This camera, this camera, this camera..."). It developed a season model, complete with finales and returning guests. It launched its own product line (The Last Dab hot sauce), spun off game shows (Truth or Dab), and built a fully branded studio around a format that never required one. What started as an internet experiment became a fully realized franchise—just not one owned by a network or greenlit by a development exec.

Today, Hot Ones is treated by celebrities and publicists as a mandatory promotional stop. Like *The Tonight Show* or *The Daily Show* in their prime, it confers cultural relevance, but the rules are inverted: it earns its legitimacy not through industry validation but through audience obsession. The platform-native talk show demonstrates that YouTube-native formats can achieve traditional media status without ever leaving their home platform.

Hot Ones succeeded by staying rooted in its native soil. It didn't jump formats or chase legacy media validation. It never needed a pitch meeting. This is the new television: not content that migrates from YouTube to legacy media, but content so compelling in its platform-native form that legacy media has no choice but to take notice.

These examples—MrBeast, Dude Perfect, Hot Ones, even the Paul brothers and Smosh—aren't outliers. They're the new networks. They mastered the core directive: hold mass attention at scale. High production values, repeatable formats, scheduled drops, tentpole events, merch empires, brand-safe spectacle. The bedroom vlog didn't disappear; it just stopped being the thing the algorithm puts on the billboard.

The result looks a lot like television, only inverted. On TV, the network owned the distribution and rented the audience to advertisers. On YouTube, the creator owns the format and the persona, but the platform still owns the pipe and the promotion. The thumbnails get louder, the hooks get faster, the niches get sanded off. To reach hundreds of millions, you have to speak in the broadest accents possible. What gets rewarded is no longer weirdness or intimacy; it's retention at any budget.

None of this is bad in itself. MrBeast is very good at what he does. Hot Ones is a brilliantly designed format. But the gravity is real: the bigger the canvas, the blunter the brush. And for every kid who watches a $10 million stunt video, there's a quieter signal getting drowned out.

Ask the actual twelve-year-olds. My son barely opens YouTube anymore. "It's boring now," he says. "The comments are mid, two or three months behind. On TikTok I hang out in the comments." That's the tell. When the second-screen conversation moves faster than the primary content, the content has already started to feel like broadcast.

This is the real cost of YouTube becoming TV: the platform that once felt like it belonged to its users now feels like it's being aired at them.

For new creators, this shift changes everything. The path to "breaking through" has become far more challenging and capital-intensive.

MrBeast's success, while inspiring, sets a nearly impossible bar. Aspiring creators aren't just competing with peers in their niche anymore—they're competing with production houses disguised as individuals, operations with dozens of employees, million-dollar budgets, and years of algorithmic refinement. The expectation for production value, conceptual ambition, and sheer scale has skyrocketed. This moves far beyond the "phone and an idea" entry point that once defined YouTube.

The professionalization of the creator economy creates opportunity for the people who can afford it. But it also rewrites what the feed is. When the top tier is basically studios dressed up as creators, the platform stops rewarding the thing it was built on. Millions can upload, sure. But the algorithm sets a bar almost no one can clear.

What gets pushed out isn't just hope. It's the odd stuff. The small, specific, human stuff. The kind of YouTube that felt like a place to hang out instead of a broadcast channel.

This intensifies the squeeze on the "middle class" creators from Chapter 3. If the top tier is now defined by broadcast-level spectacle and massive budgets, the gap between them and everyone else widens dramatically. Creators aiming for sustainable livelihoods find themselves caught in an impossible bind: optimize for an algorithm that favors scale, or remain true to a more intimate, less costly creative vision that the system increasingly refuses to surface. The new gatekeepers aren't studio executives negotiating in conference rooms—they're ranking systems demanding spectacle, enforced by capital requirements that exclude most people from the race entirely.

The shift is undeniable: the raw, unscripted bedroom vlog is giving way to the multi-million-dollar stunt.

YouTube is no longer just a platform for personal expression but a global entertainment powerhouse, driven by the same forces that shaped traditional TV—only this time, the barrier isn't a network green-light but an algorithmic one, and the cost of entry keeps climbing.

But what happens when creators try to bridge these worlds directly? The transformation of YouTube into television raises a question: if the platform has become so TV-like, shouldn't successful YouTubers be able to seamlessly transition to actual television?

Lilly Singh's story illustrates why the answer is more complex than it appears. Singh was one of YouTube's first breakout stars, building an empire on jump cuts, alter egos, and cultural commentary—content that felt personal, immediate, and feed-native. Her comedy sketches weren't just videos but rituals: consistent, creator-driven, and perfectly tuned to the rhythms of online life. She didn't need a studio, a showrunner, or a prime-time slot. YouTube gave her scale, freedom, and visibility on her own terms.

Then she made the leap. In 2019, NBC launched *A Little Late with Lilly Singh*, making her the first openly bisexual woman of color to host a network late-night show. It was framed as a cultural milestone: a YouTuber crossing into broadcast television, bringing her digital-native voice to a legacy format. But the show struggled to find its footing. The tone felt off. The structure—monologue, desk, celebrity guest—flattened Singh's energy. Her fans didn't follow her to TV, and NBC's traditional audience didn't connect with her style. What had felt intimate and immediate on YouTube became constrained and impersonal on television.

The crossover exposed a format mismatch. Singh's voice had been optimized for the platform: punchy, self-aware, emotionally elastic. Late-night TV demanded a different cadence, shaped by ad breaks, cue cards, and production routines that left little room for the improvisational honesty that made her famous.

When Singh returned to YouTube, the platform had evolved. The algorithm favored new formats, new creators, new signals. Shorts were rising. Long-form sketches were falling out of sync. Her return didn't restore the spotlight, but it reframed the lesson. The story reveals what happens when a creator tries to scale out of the feed and into legacy media, only to discover that what made her powerful was the very medium she left behind. Singh didn't fail to become a television star—television failed to become her.

This paradox reveals something important about the current moment: while YouTube has become TV-like in scale and production values, it remains different in structure, pace, and audience relationship. The creators who succeed in this new landscape aren't necessarily those who can cross over to traditional media—they're those who can harness the unique advantages of the platform while operating at broadcast scale.

If creators want to play in that territory—big budgets, brand deals, global scale—they'll need to start thinking differently, not just about the content but about the infrastructure.

TV has producers, showrunners, schedulers, and studios. Creators entering that space need strategy, structure, and support. They need to understand the system they're stepping into.

The creator economy isn't ending but evolving. And for some, the next phase really will look like television: episodic, high-production, globally distributed.

Others will go smaller, more intimate, niche and community-first. Still others will leave the platforms entirely.

What's clear is this: the creator economy doesn't just grow up but grow out. And we're watching one of those branches—the biggest, loudest one—start to harden into something familiar.

It's worth paying attention to what that branch leaves behind.

This change in how video value is created and consumed sets the stage for the next critical questions. If individual creators are being shaped into machines, and platforms are becoming the new television, who truly owns the audience? And where do viewers go when the vastness of the feed starts to feel as impersonal as broadcast has become?

6 WHO REALLY OWNS THE AUDIENCE?_

YOU RENT YOUR AUDIENCE, and the platform holds the keys.

It's tempting to see MrBeast as independent—self-made, a media empire without networks, a global brand built off-grid. But that image of independence is exactly what the system is built to produce. What appears to be creative control is, more often than not, leased scale—growth granted on the platform's terms, not yours. Even the biggest creators don't own the rails they run on. The platform does.

It's a comforting thought for any creator: I've built this. These are my fans, my followers, my people. You spend years perfecting your craft—posting, responding, refining—watching the subscriber count climb. Each spike in engagement, each milestone crossed, feels like proof of a direct connection to the people who value your work. Platforms reinforce this belief, celebrating "community," rolling out "creator tools," and talking about "your audience." It's a powerful narrative because it works. It feels like autonomy.

But that sense of ownership is an illusion. Platforms never admit it—but they treat the audience as theirs. And they are.

Platform-first ecosystems aren't neutral but powerful landlords. You, the creator, are a tenant—operating on their property, bound by shifting rules, hooked on their access to customers—the audience. You can decorate your space, attract a crowd, and even build a thriving business within their walls, but you rarely hold the deed. Your entire operation exists at their discretion, under a lease agreement few fully read or understand.

"You are the product" usually points at audiences—attention and data monetized through ads. The model is broader. Creators are products too. Platforms control the rails—distribution, monetization, rules—and rely on two inputs they don't pay to produce: content and attention. Creators supply inventory for free; audiences supply data for free. The platform sells both to advertisers.

Every upload is free inventory the platform can monetize or throttle. Every play is behavioral data the platform can package. Losing any individual creator or viewer barely dents the system; losing platform access feels existential to the creator and the user. The rental agreement isn't just about audience. It's about existence on the platform itself.

I saw early signs of this at Maker, when YouTube began tightening control under the guise of monetization tools. Since then, in my work with creators and platforms, it's only become clearer: the terms aren't just service agreements but infrastructure tilted in one direction.

Platforms own the recommendation engines that drive

discovery, the data that determines who sees what and when, the ad infrastructure, the subscriptions, the analytics dashboards. They control the APIs that gate access, the payment rails, the policies, the penalties, and ultimately, the accounts themselves.

This unseen contract lives in the Terms of Service (ToS), lengthy, dense, and rarely read legal documents that creators accept with a single click during signup. Within these pages are the subtle but powerful mechanisms that let platforms maintain control over what appears to be your audience and your content.

First, regarding content (Intellectual Property): while creators usually retain basic copyright to their original work, platforms almost universally demand broad, global, perpetual, royalty-free licenses to use, share, or tweak it. This isn't just about allowing your video to be played on their site—it means they can use your viral clip in marketing campaigns without asking for further permission or compensating you. They syndicate, repurpose, reuse—your work, their rules. They control the display and discoverability of your content, place ads, insert overlays, remove features, and reuse highlights in platform marketing or model-training without additional compensation. You see it when a clip from your channel shows up in a platform promo reel on connected TVs months later, or when a sample from your video runs inside an in-app ad for "what's trending." It's all downstream of that license. The rails belong to them, and so does the right to move your work around on those rails in ways that benefit the platform first.

Second, and perhaps more important, is control over

audience data. Platforms collect vast amounts of information on who watches what, when, and how. This isn't just basic demographics but detailed behavioral data, interest graphs, consumption patterns, and social connections across the entire platform. This trove powers highly sophisticated advertising engines and personalization algorithms. As a creator, you typically receive only aggregated, anonymized data through a dashboard—general demographics, average watch time, peak viewership times. Useful for content strategy, but still a curated, filtered view of reality—not actionable or portable in a way that lets you build an independent, resilient business. You don't get direct contact information—no emails, no phones, no lists of your loyal fans. The platform is the sole custodian of the audience relationship, guarding that direct connection as its core asset.

You feel this asymmetry most starkly on Instagram. Creators routinely report a reach drop after switching to business accounts, with paid boosts restoring visibility. Whatever the exact mechanism, the effect is clear: access to "your" followers is mediated by monetization levers. At the same time, Instagram encourages you to "build your brand" and "engage your community" while offering no formal tools for direct, off-platform communication. You can't download follower lists, segment audiences, or talk to people outside the app. The platform mediates every interaction—comments, messages, even story reach—making it nearly impossible to build a durable business beyond the feed. A platform might give advertisers robust tools to micro-target your audience with pinpoint accuracy, yet you can't micro-target those same people for your product, your subscription service, or your live event. You're given a compass but denied the map. Creators provide the content and cultivate the relationship; the platform captures the margin.

Finally, the very nature of user relationships is mediated by the platform. You can't directly email your followers outside the platform, send them a private message that bypasses its algorithms, or get a definitive list of your most loyal fans to engage with independently. Every communication, notification, and interaction passes through the platform's infrastructure, subject to its rules, moderation, and algorithmic whims. The platform is the only direct line between you and your audience, and it holds the switch.

And the walled garden isn't just about limiting creators; it's engineered to feel effortless for everyone else. One app for all the content, all the friends, all the community. That convenience is the honey around the trap: every improvement to in-app discovery and UX makes it less likely a viewer will follow you to a site, newsletter, or app you actually control. What looks like seamless product design from the outside is, for creators, another layer of lock-in.

Twitch offers a partial counterpoint. Because it's structured around live interaction, many streamers develop more direct relationships with their viewers through chat culture, mod teams, and recurring rituals. Subscribers, especially paid ones, feel more like members than followers. Yet even here, the platform owns the rails. Streamers can't export subscriber lists or payment relationships. If Twitch changed its terms tomorrow, many creators would lose the communities they spent years cultivating. The intimacy is real, and the dependency is, too.

Algorithms are the final gatekeeper. A million subscribers can become three percent reach overnight because the platform changed a weight, ran an A/B test, or decided Shorts are the new priority. Creators never see the formula—only the outcomes. The anxiety is constant, the sameness inevitable. I've watched "subscribers" or "followers" stop guaranteeing reach over and over again. Creators think they've built an audience; the algorithm quietly reminds them who decides whether that audience sees anything.

This lack of true audience ownership isn't abstract. It shows up as platform risk—channels deleted overnight, accounts suspended, livelihoods erased. It shows up as portability problems—years of accumulated audience locked inside a walled garden you can't leave without starting over. And it shows up as stunted business growth—no way to segment or contact people directly, so every new product, event, or subscription has to be pushed through someone else's funnel.

We call it the creator economy, but most creators don't own their business—they rent it on someone else's land.

Even the biggest names are often at the mercy of brand deals, platform payouts, or algorithmically determined ad revenue. YouTube's Partner Program. TikTok's Creator Fund. Instagram's bonuses. Twitch's sub splits. None of it is built for long-term control. These aren't business models but allowances, structured with one purpose: to keep creators inside the system, on-platform, dependent, compliant.

6 WHO REALLY OWNS THE AUDIENCE?

The creator's struggle for audience ownership echoes a recurring pattern throughout the history of commerce and media: battles over who controls the direct customer relationship, the source of power and value. The specifics change, but the asymmetry doesn't.

In earlier eras, newspaper and magazine publishers fiercely guarded their subscriber lists. When independent newsstands or subscription services emerged, controlling access to the reader, publishers often fought to regain direct relationships, knowing the subscriber list was their true asset.

For decades, musicians signed away control of their masters and distribution rights to labels. Labels, in turn, controlled fan clubs and direct marketing. Artists often fought for years to regain control of their music and, crucially, their direct relationship with fans, knowing the label's power came from mediating that connection.

In the early days of the internet, companies like AOL built "walled gardens" for access, trying to control everything a user did online. They curated content, provided email, and built communities within their own ecosystem. The open web eventually broke these monopolies. Today's platforms are modern versions of this old ambition to control the entire user journey and relationship.

These historical examples underscore that the battle for audience ownership is timeless. What makes the current iteration unique is its sheer scale, algorithmic opacity, and the individual creator's relative powerlessness against monolithic platforms. And that asymmetry is about to get worse, because AI doesn't just preserve this system—it intensifies it.

AI doesn't change who owns the audience. It changes how little anyone else matters.

Platforms don't need to replace creators with synthetic characters. The bottom tier is already free. Millions of people are making content for nothing or close to it, feeding the machine in the hope that something hits. The problem, from a platform's point of view, isn't the long tail. It's what happens when some of those creators succeed and start to gain leverage—when they become expensive.

That's where AI comes in.

First, AI floods the bottom. Tools that generate "good enough" thumbnails, hooks, scripts, even entire videos mean there's always more inventory. You don't need a studio or a team; you need a prompt and a phone. The feed fills with AI-assisted clips at almost no marginal cost. There's always someone—or something—willing to post more often for less.

At the same time, AI compresses the service layer around creators. Editing, thumbnails, copy, basic analytics—work that used to cost $30–$100 an hour collapses into $20–$50-a-month software. Seventy-percent quality becomes cheap and ubiquitous. Top creators still hire human teams for best-in-class work. For everyone else, "professional-looking" is now the default, not the differentiator.

That squeeze hits the middle hardest. Creators making $50,000–$150,000 a year once justified small teams to outrun the pack on polish and cadence. Now the bottom has AI-assisted polish, and the top uses AI to scale further. View distribution concentrates. CPMs sag as supply spikes. More creators report working more hours for the same or less return. The middle class we keep being promised is exactly where the pressure concentrates.

And then the system takes the next step.

The platform captures the spread. More inventory from the bottom. Cheaper production in the middle. Bigger tentpoles at the top—all competing for attention the platform already controls. The creator brings the human element. AI brings the labor compression. The platform keeps the margin. AI doesn't flip the power dynamic; it accelerates it.

Then comes the part that looks like nirvana from the platform's side: fungibility.

Feeds fill with faceless compilations, AI-voiced listicles, remixable templates, trend-driven Shorts and Reels where "who made this?" is an irrelevant question. Human creators and AI systems compete in the same pool. At the bottom, humans are effectively free. At the top, anyone who becomes expensive—anyone who starts to matter—faces near-free AI competition nipping at their heels. Identity stops being a moat; it becomes an optional layer the platform can route around.

AI doesn't just add more content; it learns from what already works. The more successful you are, the more you teach the system how to copy you. Hooks, pacing, color palettes, camera moves, joke structures—the patterns that built your audience become training data for a machine that can spin out infinite "close enough" variants without sleep, benefits, or negotiation. From a viewer's perspective, it all blurs into "more of what I like." From the platform's perspective, it's a way to satisfy that demand without letting any single creator become indispensable.

You can already see this logic taking shape in music. Spotify spent a decade training listeners to follow playlists, moods, and mixes instead of artists, turning songs into interchangeable units that serve "focus," "chill," or "study" more than any individual voice. Now labels like Universal are cutting deals with AI music engines trained on their own catalogs, promising a new "music creation and streaming platform" built from licensed back catalog and synthetic tracks. You don't need a human to write the next perfect background song if you can synthesize a close-enough version from the data you already own. For most listeners, if it sounds like Kenny G, it might as well be Kenny G—right up until it's time to cut the check. The more listening shifts to "Play something like this," the easier it is for the system to route plays toward whoever is cheapest to pay, and away from whoever just became expensive.

Video is on the same path. If Shorts and Reels train you to swipe for "more like this," the platform doesn't care whether the next clip comes from the creator you followed, a smaller creator mimicking them, or an AI system stitching together the pattern. To the viewer, it's all one river. To the platform, it's a pricing problem: fill the feed with the mix of human and synthetic work that maximizes time spent and minimizes obligation. As AI gets better at emulating the top performers, success stops being a moat and starts being a blueprint for your future competition.

That's the real function of AI in a platform-first ecosystem. It's not there to replace the free labor at the bottom. It's there to cap the power of anyone who rises too far above it. As soon as a creator looks less like a tenant and more like a negotiating counterparty, the system can point to a universe of cheaper alternatives—some human, some synthetic—and quietly remind them who owns the audience, and who can be swapped out.

Platform-first ecosystems reveal the missing piece: true audience ownership. What would it look like to reverse that?

A few creators have figured it out, not the most viral ones but the ones who've taken control of their infrastructure. They build email lists, own their domain, and direct fans to paid communities. They treat platforms as top-of-funnel, not as home base. They use Patreon, Discord, Shopify, or their own apps. They get audience insight, not just impressions.

Audience ownership doesn't follow a fixed formula. Some creators build massive engines that mirror TV studios. Others build intimate ecosystems that function more like clubs or collectives. What matters isn't scale or tone but control. Below are two very different paths to the same outcome: sovereignty over the audience you've earned.

Dhar Mann makes morality plays. Short, scripted videos engineered for repeatability and maximum emotional manipulation at minimum cost. The acting is stiff, the dialogue obvious, the plots predictable, the lessons delivered with the subtlety of a public-service announcement. But the output is relentless, and the results are undeniable: more than 20 billion views, 60+ million followers across platforms, a production studio, a merch empire, and a mobile app that lets him bypass algorithms entirely.

The key isn't taste or polish. It's ownership. He controls the entire stack: writing, casting, production, distribution, monetization, and the direct-to-fan relationship. Formats are vertically integrated and relentlessly repeatable, so cash flow is predictable and the audience always knows exactly what it's getting. This isn't just creator success. It's creator-as-network, built to outlive any single platform.

And yes, the content is the lowest-dollar version of cable television: blunt morality tales wrapped in fake virtue. That's the point. Even that works, spectacularly, when you own the factory.

If Dhar Mann built a fortress, the Sorry Girls built a village. They did not chase viral trends but built a creative home. As a DIY and lifestyle brand launched on YouTube, Kelsey and Becky cultivated a tone that felt more like a friend's living room than a content studio. Projects were aspirational but accessible, humor self-deprecating, aesthetic cohesive. Over time, their channel did not just grow but became a space people wanted to return to.

What they did next mattered even more. Instead of funneling their audience into brand deals or algorithmic scale, they built infrastructure: a newsletter, a merch line, a blog, and eventually a paid Discord server. It is a higher-touch model that scales more slowly and demands ongoing participation from the creators themselves. Each piece deepened the relationship and filtered for intent. The path from YouTube video to inbox to Discord was not organic drift but funnel design. Each step required higher trust, higher engagement, and higher willingness to pay.

They understood that audience is not just a number but a network, and that ownership is not only about monetization but about retention architecture. Community was not an afterthought but the product. But building it required the same structural discipline Mann applied to content: consistent tone, deliberate pacing, and format guardrails their audience could rely on. "Aspirational but accessible" is not accidental but a carefully maintained brand position.

Where platforms reward velocity, the Sorry Girls chose depth, a trade-off that caps scale but increases durability. Slower growth means smaller addressable markets, with intimacy constraining reach. That is not a flaw but a design constraint they navigated intentionally. And where many creators built content engines, they built a brand with owned touchpoints at every layer. They reduced platform dependency by building direct lines that can travel across formats and partners. The trade-off is maintenance: community is durable, but it must be tended.

Ownership in this context isn't a manifesto. It looks like a direct line off-platform you can actually use, identity and billing that travel across surfaces you control, a community that can migrate without breaking, and practical control over where your work appears and how it's packaged. When those conditions hold, the power balance shifts, even if you still publish inside the gardens. And once you can reach people directly, you can finally build discovery around human intent instead of platform habit.

The audience never really belonged to the platform in the first place. They came for you. But when creators don't know their audience—when the relationship is mediated by algorithmic black boxes—they can't serve them effectively. They create for the feed instead of for actual human needs. That disconnect is why, despite infinite content, we're all struggling to find what we want to watch. It isn't just a technical failure. The discovery crisis is what happens when a system severs the connection between creators and the people who showed up for them in the first place.

7 INFRASTRUCTURE IS THE NEW STAR SYSTEM_

IN THE OLD MEDIA ORDER, power had a face. The star—singular, magnetic, relentlessly promoted—was the axis around which entire industries turned, with visibility, financing, and distribution all flowing through them and bending around them. But the real power was never just in the performance; it lived in the machine behind the scenes with the programmers, the marketers, the tastemakers, the dealmakers. The star system wasn't simply about charisma; it was a model of controlled visibility that for decades set the rules for who rose, who mattered, and who got seen.

That architecture didn't vanish. It evolved. The machinery that once manufactured stars is now embedded in platforms, feeds, algorithms, and infrastructure, with human selectors replaced by systems. And the new system doesn't reward the most original voice or the most dedicated work—in the modern attention economy, it's not the best content that wins, it's the best distribution. You don't see a recommendation engine, you see a face, while the system sees lanes, deadlines, and budgets: who gets routed where, and how often—across phones, TVs, and every home screen that now sits between creator and audience.

The early creator economy promised to flatten the hierarchy, claiming anyone could break through and spontaneity and authenticity could outshine polish and precision in what felt almost anarchic. But as we saw earlier, that promise collapsed into a power law where only a sliver of creators rise, and even fewer endure. Those who do—MrBeast, Rhett & Link, the Paul brothers—succeed not on charisma alone, but on what surrounds them, because behind every mega-creator is a machine with teams, tools, analytics, and capital. The star system didn't disappear, it migrated, and infrastructure, not celebrity, is now the engine of scale.

This shift—from charisma to coordination, from solo acts to structured systems—isn't always visible to audiences, but for creators trying to scale, infrastructure is the revolution shaping the next phase of the economy. Understanding how it works explains why some creators break through, and why others burn out.

The typical creator journey starts as a solo endeavor with one person, an idea, a camera, and a drive to connect. They handle everything—ideation, scripting, filming, editing, uploading, community management, marketing, monetization—and it's celebrated as the essence of independence, but it's also a bottleneck. As the audience grows, success becomes its own trap because the creative work that drew them in gets crowded out by the weight of operational demands.

I've watched this transition repeatedly in my advisory

work, with creators coming to me when they hit the operational wall, when the work finally outruns them. They're drowning in administrative tasks, missing brand opportunities because they can't respond fast enough, or burning out from trying to be everywhere at once, and the ones who break through make a conscious decision to stop trying to do everything and start building systems to handle what they can't.

Today, creators are expected to do it all—you're the talent, the brand, the editor, the strategist, the account manager, the analyst, the producer, the community lead, all while being scalable and spontaneous, independent and omnipresent, authentic but optimized, always on. That expectation isn't just exhausting, it's structurally unsustainable, because the lone genius with a webcam quickly collides with the reality of administrative overload. The more successful a video, the more it demands, with comments to moderate, brands to manage, analytics to parse, follow-ups to plan, creating a cycle where the very success you wanted becomes the engine of collapse. It's celebrated as independence, but it's really an overload loop—the Platform Factory's first test.

TikTok complicates this by offering creators a low-friction path to virality, placing them one video, one sound, one trend away from massive exposure. But virality almost never becomes infrastructure, and even creators with millions of followers struggle to monetize or sustain their audience because TikTok rewards immediacy, not longevity. Without operational systems, most success stories flame out as quickly as they rose.

For a select few, the path diverges when they realize

that to scale, to turn a hobby into a business, they must shed the illusion of the solo act and build infrastructure. This isn't just about hiring an editor, it's about creating systems, processes, and a distributed team that lets the core creative talent focus on what only they can do—be the face, the voice, the unique personality—and the transition from "creator" to "founder" of a media enterprise is a conscious, strategic leap.

Rhett & Link show how this evolution works. Early Good Mythical Morning episodes were just the two of them in front of a camera, a simple, homespun setup, but today, Mythical Entertainment is a multichannel enterprise with staff covering everything from segment R&D to merch design, legal, HR, and syndication. They operate out of a sprawling studio complex, managing a portfolio of shows, podcasts, and even a fan club, no longer just two guys with a show but the visible front of a sophisticated media company, orchestrating a complex ecosystem of content and commerce.

MrBeast's elaborate stunts—recreating Squid Game, giving away private jets—aren't possible without dozens of full-time employees handling project management and logistics, building immersive sets, shaping narrative through editing, and tracking performance through strategic analysis. This isn't just a YouTube channel, it's a full-scale production house, engineered for maximum reach and impact, because scale without structure is a trap. The demands of millions of viewers, nonstop content cycles, and diversified revenue require operational infrastructure that can withstand pressure and evolve quickly.

7 INFRASTRUCTURE IS THE NEW STAR SYSTEM

Twitch streamers offer a parallel case, with many starting with just a webcam and OBS, but at the top tier, streams are run by teams including mods, chat managers, live producers, VOD editors, sponsorship managers, even business analysts. What looks spontaneous is often tightly choreographed, and behind the ease of interaction is infrastructure that mirrors live television more than it does solo content creation.

This new star system of infrastructure takes many forms, often invisible to the casual viewer. A growing ecosystem of fractional professionals and specialized agencies now supports creators, turning what was once an impossible overhead into a flexible, scalable cost, and this support is a far cry from the one-size-fits-all approach of the old Multi-Channel Networks (MCNs) that often stifled creators. Today, it's about customization, targeted support for creator-led businesses.

Here's what that infrastructure actually looks like when you pull the camera back. The help arrives in fragments—an editor in Manila who turns twelve hours into three, a community lead who answers four hundred DMs without sounding like a bot, a brand wrangler who turns a vague "collab?" into terms, timelines, and a wire date, a strategist who moves a cold open six seconds and buys two extra points of retention, a merch partner who eats the inventory risk so cash flow doesn't break the month—and none of them are on camera, all of them are on the clock. They're the difference between "post whenever it's done" and an actual release calendar that can live on both YouTube and the living-room app without breaking.

Cash tells its own story with platform payouts hitting

net-30 or net-60, meaning one missed week starves the next, while brands pay on delivery and COGS for a hoodie lands up front unless a partner floats it. Distribution has clocks too, with long-form Thursday, cut-downs to VOD by Sunday, Shorts seeding the arc all week, and none of it appears in the upload while all of it decides whether the next one happens.

Beyond human support, the infrastructure includes a growing suite of sophisticated technology and tools that act as digital force multipliers. That ranges from advanced analytics platforms that dissect audience behavior in detail, offering insights far beyond native dashboards, to specialized production software for complex visual effects or sound design, along with custom Customer Relationship Management (CRM) systems to manage brand relationships and track outreach. Internal project management systems keep multi-person teams aligned on complex content pipelines, ensuring timely delivery, and these are the digital levers that allow a handful of people to achieve output that once required an entire studio, streamlining workflows and amplifying efficiency.

The most invisible layer covers the behind-the-scenes operations that ensure financial and legal stability, including legal support for drafting contracts, managing intellectual property, and navigating copyright issues—necessary in a world where content is constantly sampled and remixed—along with rigorous accounting and financial management for complex revenue streams from multiple platforms, brand deals, and direct fan support. Human resources functions for growing teams handle hiring, payroll, and team dynamics, and these unglamorous elements allow a creative individual to operate like a sustainable business.

Live commerce streams show what happens when you wire creator, identity, payment, and ritual into one closed loop. Platforms like TikTok Shop are already reporting conversion rates as high as 30%, compared to the 2–3% that's considered healthy for traditional e-commerce. It's not just influencer marketing 2.0. It's a system where the "show" is a storefront, the "episode" is a buying ritual, and the real asset is the infrastructure that holds them together. When the pipes are engineered end-to-end—when discovery, transaction, and return all happen in the same room—you get a completely different economic profile. This isn't the future most legacy media is building toward. It's the system discovering that ritual, properly instrumented, converts.

The myth of the solo genius persists, but successful creators are surrounded by an invisible network of operators and systems. What most platforms won't say, and most fans don't see, is that successful creators are already running businesses, with some not realizing it and others trying to deny it. But the creators who last, the ones who move from volatility to viability, embrace it.

Like any business, creators need infrastructure—not followers, not better content, not another algorithm hack, but strategy, operations, talent, finance, legal, partnerships, and systems.

We don't talk about this enough because it breaks the mythology, since we like to imagine creators as solo acts. But behind every long-term creator business, there's a team, fractional or full-time, visible or invisible, providing a layer of support that keeps the machine running while the creator performs, and that's not selling out, that's staying in.

This shift toward infrastructure marks an evolution in the creator economy's value chain. In the first wave, content was king and personality was its champion, but now, the operational processes that enable the creation and distribution of that content have become equally, if not more, valuable.

Operationally, that shift shows up most clearly in cadence. Think about the challenge of consistent output when platforms reward frequency and reliability. For a solo creator, hitting a weekly upload schedule with high-quality content is a huge task, often leading to creative exhaustion and a drop in quality, but for a creator with a well-oiled machine of editors, animators, and researchers, consistency becomes the natural result of a well-designed process. Their "star power" is now as much about operational excellence as personal charisma, with the reliability of their content delivery, the seamlessness of their brand integrations, and the professional management of their community all contributing to a perceived level of quality that translates into sustained audience engagement and business opportunities.

And once that machinery meets algorithmic demand, a darker thing happens: it makes creators better factory inputs. While algorithms push for sameness and reward those who can churn out optimized content, creators with robust infrastructure are better equipped to meet these demands without burning out or sacrificing their unique voice, able to pivot formats, chase trending topics, or

7 INFRASTRUCTURE IS THE NEW STAR SYSTEM   119

significantly increase output because they have the operational capacity to do so. They become more efficient "automata" within the factory, not by sacrificing their unique voice, but by building a mechanism around it that meets the system's demands, which is why creators need operators—scale without structure is a trap, leading to burnout and missed opportunities. The true value often lies not just in the initial creative spark, but in the repeatable, optimized process that lets that spark consistently reach millions and generate sustainable revenue.

One example is Jet Lag: The Game, a YouTube series that thrives not on creator celebrity but on smart, scalable design. Its creators have engineered a repeatable format—a travel competition across time zones, optimized for serialized storytelling and retention—with the stakes, pacing, and structure calibrated to serve both audience enjoyment and YouTube's recommendation engine. Their success isn't an accident of virality or charisma, it's operational fluency applied to storytelling, packaging routes as carefully as stories, with hooks for "Up Next," clips that travel, and end-cards that hand you to the next leg. Jet Lag wins not because YouTube "picked" it, but because the format is engineered to travel: clipped cleanly into Shorts, serialized into seasons, and legible enough that it could sit as a FAST (free ad-supported streaming TV) channel block tomorrow without changing its DNA.

Look at the most enduring figures in creator media—they didn't just make great videos, they built systems including well-defined content pipelines that ensure a steady stream of engaging material, sophisticated merchandise strategies that turn fan loyalty into profitable product lines, intricate licensing deals that expand their intellectual property beyond a single platform, and structured IP frameworks that protect their creations and allow for future diversification. They built frameworks to support the creativity, not replace it, and these systems are the unseen intellectual property that fuels their long-term viability, far more valuable than any fleeting viral hit.

And those frameworks are run by a new class of operators who are not merely assistants—they are fractional executives, creative producers, revenue strategists, and advisors. They are seasoned professionals with expertise in traditional media, cutting-edge technology, and modern commerce, now plugging into creator businesses the way a Chief Operating Officer might plug into a rapidly scaling startup, bringing strategic foresight, operational discipline, and industry connections that no solo creator could ever amass.

This isn't the return of the MCN model, it's the opposite, because MCNs were about aggregation, signing hundreds of creators and taking a large cut for often generalized, limited support. This is about customization—tailored support for creator-led businesses, focused on their unique needs and long-term vision—and the conversation isn't "how do we monetize your channel" in a generic sense, but "how do we build something real with you, and around you," something that transcends a single platform or content type.

Some of this work happens quietly, behind the scenes, within the creator's own burgeoning enterprise, while some of it is built into newer firms and agencies that specialize in creator services. But the trend is clear—the most valuable resource in the creator economy isn't just reach, it's operational fluency, the ability to build, manage, and evolve the systems that transform creative output into a sustainable, scalable business.

When the machine misfires, it's rarely taste, it's structure, because cadence outruns capacity and quality slides. Evergreen revenue promises eat margin long after the lift is done, a warehouse built for one hot quarter turns into drag, and an exclusivity clause blocks the surfaces that grow the next format. The audience blames the video, but the P&L tells the story.

This new reality presents both a challenge and an insight for aspiring creators as the landscape professionalizes and the rules of the game change.

First, the cost of entry is rising again. While it may still seem "free" to start a channel with just a phone and an internet connection, building something scalable and sustainable takes more than talent—it requires capital to hire a team or the savvy to attract investors and skilled fractional talent. The romanticized "bootstrapped superstar" who stumbles into virality is being replaced by the "bootstrapped entrepreneur" who understands leverage and builds systems from day one, and the field is no longer leveled by access to tech, it's tiered by access to infrastructure. Those who can command resources will keep pulling ahead. This is how the power law hardens: not just through algorithmic bias, but through infrastructure access—who can afford the machine.

Second, a new skill set is paramount, because success is no longer just about artistic talent or compelling personality, it's about mastering business operations, team management, and strategic outsourcing. The ideal creator isn't just a brilliant artist, they're a mini-CEO who understands financial models, marketing funnels, legal frameworks, and how to delegate effectively.

This raises the barrier for the middle, with creators who can't afford, attract, or assemble this infrastructure remaining stuck in low-income, high-effort loops—burning out while the top tier pulls further ahead, buoyed by invisible support systems. Their inability to scale operations becomes as limiting as their inability to gain algorithmic favor, leaving them vulnerable and often disillusioned as the chasm between professionalized creator businesses and everyone else widens.

The creator economy's transformation isn't just about new stars, it's about the rise of operational systems that enable scale, and the next wave of breakouts won't be defined by charisma alone but by the infrastructure behind them. Those who master this new star system will shape the future of digital content.

Strip the faces off the thumbnails and what remains is process, because the channels that endure don't just make more, they move better—ideas into shoots, shoots into edits, edits into packages that travel on schedules the platforms can reward. Infrastructure is the new star system because it converts volatility into reliability, and that, more than charisma, is what keeps a creator seen.

8 ONE IS THE LONELIEST NUMBER_

THE LIVING ROOM TV used to have a clear identity. It was the family screen, the shared space, the place where everyone gathered to watch the same thing at the same time. What played there was television—professionally produced, broadly appealing, designed for communal viewing. The remote controlled which channel, but the channel controlled what you watched.

Then streaming arrived and promised liberation: watch what you want, when you want, on your terms. The TV became a portal to infinite libraries, algorithmically personalized, optimized for individual taste. The infrastructure powering that experience—recommendation engines, user profiles, watch history tracking—were all designed around a singular assumption: one person, one screen, one set of preferences.

But the living room TV never stopped being a shared device. YouTube, born on phones and laptops as the domain of individual creators and niche passions, is now the most-watched app on connected TVs. TikTok, designed for vertical scrolling on a six-inch screen, is pushing into the living room. Netflix, Hulu, and Disney+ sit alongside them in the same grid. Social media content that started on personal devices now competes with premium streaming on the biggest screen in the house, and the algorithms meant to serve individuals are now trying to serve groups—families, couples, roommates—on a device where "who's watching" is rarely singular and almost never stable.

This is where phone-native content and TV-native content converge. They share the same glass, the same home screen, the same recommendation rows. But the infrastructure underneath them was never designed for communal viewing. It's optimized for one: one profile, one algorithm, one set of assumptions about taste. The result isn't just broken discovery—it's discovery that collapses worst in the space where it matters most.

The scenario is familiar: Friday night, you and your partner on the couch, remote in hand, trying to find something to watch. You open the first streaming app, then the second, then the third, scrolling through endless rows of thumbnails—'New Release,' 'Trending Now,' 'Critically Acclaimed Dramas.' You see a hundred options, but none of them feel right. Your partner suggests something, you counter with another, and the conversation loops while twenty minutes bleed into thirty, then forty-five. Eventually, exhausted by the friction of choosing, you default to re-watching an old favorite, or you simply give up.

In our house, when I hit that wall—tired, uninspired, scrolling through apps with nothing jumping out—I often

8 ONE IS THE LONELIEST NUMBER

default to T2, the Tennis Channel, the FAST channel that boots up automatically on our Samsung TV, not really choosing it but letting it run as a placeholder, ambient and frictionless, until inspiration arrives, if it ever does.

My wife takes the opposite route, moving quickly and scanning Netflix or Hulu for something familiar enough to feel safe but new enough to hold her interest. And our 12-year-old skips the TV entirely, never even opening the guide if he's alone, with YouTube or TikTok as his starting points—not the end of the search, but the beginning.

These aren't quirks of personality. They're three different coping strategies for the same underlying problem: systems built for individual optimization failing at communal context. When the TV tries to serve everyone, it ends up serving no one.

The problem isn't a lack of content, or even a lack of good content. It's that the systems connecting us to that content were designed for a different use case entirely. They assume singular identity, stable preferences, and uninterrupted individual viewing. The living room TV breaks all three assumptions, but the infrastructure hasn't caught up.

For decades, finding something to watch was straightforward with a handful of television channels, a printed TV guide, or a weekly trip to Blockbuster. Choice was limited, but discovery was simple, and often communal. You picked a channel, flipped through a few options, or trusted the recommendation of a friend or a movie critic. Scarcity doubled as a filter and built a shared cultural watercooler around a few key programs.

Now, every person carries a supercomputer in their

pocket, connected to a global network offering millions of films, billions of videos, and an unending stream of digital creations. On paper, that should be utopia. In practice, when that abundance pours through the living room TV, the experience often feels less like strolling through a curated gallery and more like rummaging through an overstuffed closet with someone standing next to you waiting for a decision. Access doesn't equal discovery. The old tools were bus schedules—check what's arriving at 8 p.m. and decide. The new ones still act like everything runs on someone else's timetable.

For creators, this isn't merely a nuisance but an existential problem. When audiences can't find you, you can't grow. When they can't rediscover you, your work doesn't last. And when they don't land on your content at the precise moment it resonates, you don't get paid. Discovery is really about connection—finding something that feels timely, personal, and frictionless, even when you didn't know you were looking for it. But when the systems can't tell who's in the room or why they pressed play, connection becomes a matter of luck.

Zoom out and the pattern is obvious.

Recommendation engines were sold as guides that would surface hidden gems. Early on, they sometimes did. Over time the job changed: no longer "help you find what you want," but "keep you here longer." The engines adapted. They became very good at predicting what generates the next hour of watch time and much worse at understanding mood, company, or intent. A single kids' cartoon watched with a niece can derail an adult profile for weeks.

It doesn't care why something was watched, only that it was. From the platform's standpoint this is efficient. From the couch—where two or three people are trying to agree—it's the opposite of helpful.

TikTok weaponizes that logic. A few extra seconds of attention on one kind of clip become a vote for an entire category, then an entire mood. TikTok didn't invent that math—reckoning by tonnage, where every second watched is treated as proof of desire—but it runs the loop in real time, turning the feed itself into a factory floor where every second of watch time is another adjustment of the machine. Watch a handful of home-improvement videos and your entire feed pivots. Linger on one melancholy post and you're in a spiral of sadness. What looks like personalization is often just reactive standardization, tuned for retention rather than resonance.

The gap between behavior and intent becomes especially dangerous when a few seconds of watch time on a controversial clip can poison the algorithm for weeks. The platform sees every micro-interaction as signal but it lacks context—not knowing if you were hate-watching, doomscrolling, or just curious. TikTok's engine logs a three-second linger as affinity even when it's rubbernecking.

On a phone, that's annoying. On a shared TV, it's lethal. One stray spiral from one person tilts the whole home screen. A kid's five-minute Minecraft binge, your partner's true-crime detour, a guest's random rabbit hole—suddenly the room inherits a mood nobody asked for. Friday night becomes a negotiation with yesterday's accidental clicks.

And then there's the "black box" problem. We rarely

understand why we're being shown what we're shown. The recommendations arrive as cryptic pronouncements, without explanation or rationale. But opacity is also strategic—if you can't see the levers, you can't argue with them. When it consistently gets it wrong, or when it reinforces our existing biases without introducing anything truly novel, we stop trusting it. The once-promised personalization turns into a monotonous echo chamber, where every recommendation feels like a slightly different shade of what we've already seen. The algorithms have gotten smarter at predicting what will keep us watching next, but dumber at helping us find what we actually want in the room we're sitting in. That's not a bug. That's an alignment choice.

If recommendation engines are the factory's conveyor belt, two older tools—EPGs (Electronic Program Guides) and search—are the front doors. And they have their own quiet misalignments.

They're one-person front doors on a many-person room.

Imagine you're not alone with a laptop but standing in front of the TV with someone else, trying to find something to watch together. EPGs were bus schedules, plain and simple: here's what's pulling in at 8 p.m., get on or wait for the next one. You flipped through a hundred channels, saw what was on now or coming up, and made a choice. It solved a simple problem: what's on tonight?

But in a world of infinite, on-demand content, the EPG feels outdated. When a single streaming service can offer thousands of films and series, and a single creator can have a library of hundreds of videos, what exactly does a "program guide" show—a grid of thousands of empty slots, a scrollable wall of text so vast it's unnavigable? The EPG was never designed for discovery but for navigation when you already knew the landscape. It's still good at the platform's job—advertising inventory and showing you what they have to sell you tonight—not at your job, which is figuring out what makes sense right now, in this room, with these people.

Then there's search. If the EPG is the aisle, search is walking up to the counter and saying, "I need X. Do you have it? Which version? Where is it?" The search bar, a digital godsend in the world of facts and information retrieval, becomes a blunt instrument in the realm of subjective taste. When you don't know what you're looking for, or when you're trying to discover something new based on a mood or a feeling—or someone else's mood or feeling—traditional keyword search comes up short. You can't search for "something funny but also thought-provoking, that's not too long and I haven't seen before, and my partner will like."

Think about the Netflix search bar and how often you actually use it effectively, beyond looking up a specific title you already know about. Type in "comedy," and you get a deluge of every comedy ever made, from slapstick to dark humor, without any real sense of hierarchy or nuance, and no sense of which one fits tonight with the person sitting next to you. It's optimized for retrieval when you have clear intent, but offers almost no help when your intent is vague, shared, or driven by serendipity. Search is a precise tool for known knowns. Discovery in the living room lives in the unknowns. From the platform's perspective, that's fine:

search confirms inventory and closes demand. From yours, it leaves most of the real problem unsolved.

Beyond the algorithms and the broken tools, the very design of streaming interfaces has made the discovery crisis worse. What was once intended to be intuitive and empowering has become a labyrinth designed for endless scrolling, not genuine connection. The user experience of streaming has collapsed under the weight of its own content.

Navigate any major streaming service today, and you are met with an overwhelming visual assault of endless horizontal rows of content, categorized by generic, often unhelpful labels like "Action & Adventure," "Comedies," "New Releases," "Trending Now," "Because You Watched X." The categories are too broad to be useful in a world of millions of titles, where "Comedy" could be anything from a classic sitcom to a raunchy stand-up special to a dark, satirical film, with little to no human curation and no sense of hierarchy beyond what the algorithm is currently trying to push.

This leads directly to endless scrolling and joint decision fatigue. You and the person next to you aren't just choosing a show; you're negotiating taste, mood, and time, with the interface offering almost no help beyond "more." In the streaming world, that often ends with one of two outcomes: rewatch a show you've both seen a dozen times, or abandon the pursuit altogether. The screen that was supposed to make things easier just made the room feel heavier.

But again: from the platform's vantage point, this isn't entirely a failure. An interface that keeps you inside the app, bouncing between rails and almost deciding, is still time-on-platform. The carousel that feels like noise to you is a perfectly tuned marketing surface to them.

Much of this UX is driven by platform-centric design, not user-centric discovery. The primary goal of the streaming service's interface is to keep you within their walled garden, consuming their content. The home screen isn't a personalized guide to the best content across the entire ecosystem but a billboard for the platform's latest originals, the shows they've invested billions in and desperately need you to watch. The emphasis is on marketing, on pushing the platform's agenda, rather than genuinely helping you find the most relevant or satisfying thing for this room, on this night—even if it lives on a competitor's service or comes from an independent creator.

The lack of meaningful social or communal features in many modern streaming UX further isolates the viewer. Historically, discovery was often a social act. You watched what your friends were talking about, what critics were raving about, what was discussed at the office water cooler. Recommendations came from trusted sources, embedded in a social context. While online communities exist, they are often disconnected from the primary viewing experience, and the modern streaming UX often isolates the viewer, making discovery a solitary, algorithmically driven endeavor, even when two or three people are sitting on the couch.

The platforms powering today's streaming landscape were built for individuals navigating personal screens. They tracked what you watched, learned your patterns, and tried to predict what you'd watch next. That logic worked reasonably well when YouTube lived on laptops and phones, when Netflix was something you watched alone on a tablet, when TikTok was a vertical feed you scrolled in bed.

Now the same stack runs on the TV, but the room didn't change. The algorithm can't tell if it's you, your partner, your kids, or all of you together. It can't distinguish between Tuesday night alone and Saturday afternoon with the family. It still treats every session as if it's serving one person with one stable set of preferences, when in reality it's serving a rotating cast with conflicting tastes and shifting contexts.

The platforms know this. They've introduced profiles, Kids Mode, "Who's Watching?" prompts. But those are patches, not solutions. Profiles require manual switching, which adds friction most people skip. Kids Mode is a gate, not a contextual system. And even when you do switch profiles, the algorithm still treats each one as a singular, stable identity—it doesn't know that "your" profile on Friday night (alone, unwinding) is a completely different viewer than "your" profile on Sunday morning (with a seven-year-old, needing something light).

This is where discovery doesn't just fail—it collapses. The problem isn't that the technology is unsophisticated. It's that the assumptions baked into that technology are fundamentally mismatched to how the device is actually used. You can build the world's best recommendation engine, the smartest content-matching algorithm, the most elegant UI, and it will still fail if it's trying to serve a group as if they were one person.

Discovery is broken everywhere. But it's broken worst where it matters most: the room where people actually gather. The living room isn't one person. The system still thinks it is. Which raises the obvious question: what happens if you build for the room instead of the platform?

PART 3
AFFILIATION_

The creator economy didn't stall—it calcified as platforms professionalized, tools matured, and playbooks standardized. What began open and improvisational now runs like a machine. The tighter the system gets, the more energy leaks at the edges. That's where the next wave forms.

The cable bundle didn't die with streaming; it dissolved into algorithms—reassembling as invisible rows, autoplay queues, and personalized feeds. "Streaming" and "social" aren't just blurring. They're merging into one continuous flow of attention. In a world where content is infinite and attention is finite, value shifts from owning to organizing, from distribution control to discovery design, from shows to channels, from interface to identity, from profiles to rooms.

These chapters move from critique to build. Chapter 9 asks what would change if we put the audience first instead of the catalog—designing discovery around who's in the room, what they're trying to do, and why they're there at all. Chapter 10 shifts the unit of value from individual hits to channels: human-curated lanes built for return, not one-off spikes. Chapter 11 goes under the interface to the "who," arguing that identity—fluid, contextual, often collective—is the missing variable in every recommendation system we have. Chapter 12 adds ritual and return: cadence, clocks, and rooms people come back to on purpose, turning rented attention into durable affiliation.

The signals are here already: creators leaving static feeds for curated channels; audiences selecting by identity state, not just genre; rituals turning viewers into members. A syndication layer is taking shape, and the future belongs to organizers of relevance—people who can route attention with trust into channels and spaces that feel like theirs.

This isn't nostalgia. It's building what's native to now—grounded in how people actually live, connect, and return. Power won't just move from platforms to creators; it will move to the communities they serve and the systems that keep them together. The open question is whether we design for extraction—or for affiliation.

9 WHAT IF WE PUT THE AUDIENCE FIRST?_

IN THE LAST CHAPTER, we watched the living room TV expose the lie at the center of the modern media machine: everything has been built for one person, on one screen, with one stable set of preferences. The most important screen in the house has never worked that way. It's shared, negotiated, constantly shifting. The systems are optimized for a single viewer. The room is not, which raises the obvious question: what happens if you build for the room instead of the platform?

The current stack asks a narrow question—how do we keep you here?—and answers it with every tool at its disposal. An audience-first stack starts from a broader, more human one: who's here, what are they trying to do, and how do we help them get there with as little friction as possible? Same screens, same pipes, different job.

That sounds abstract until you flip the camera back around. A platform-first system stares at the feed and optimizes for time-on-platform. An audience-first system looks into the room. Two adults who finally got the kids down and have forty quiet minutes. A parent and a seven-year-old on a Sunday morning looking for "safe, light, and not irritating." A group of friends half-talking, half-watching something they can dip in and out of. Someone alone on a Tuesday night who wants to be challenged, not comforted. Right now, all of those show up as the same "user." The machine treats them as one person with one set of preferences. Audience-first discovery starts by admitting they aren't.

When you work backward from those situations instead of the session length, you arrive at a different set of pressures. It stops being a question of which row to spotlight and becomes a question of how much work you're forcing people to do before they can relax. And if this system actually worked for the audience, four design requirements would show up every time: real control over what's happening to them; a way to show up differently in different contexts without starting over; a filter they can trust between them and the firehose; and a system that cares why they're there, not just what they pressed last. Agency, identity, trust, intent: four places where the current infrastructure keeps failing the room.

In a platform-first world, "personalization" is something done to you. You open an app and it announces who you are today based on a trail of clicks you barely remember leaving. There are thumbs, stars, and "Not Interested" buttons, but most of the time they feel like placebo controls; you tap, nothing visible happens, and the next night the same tile returns or its cousin does.

An audience-first system would make that cause and effect visible. "More like this," "less like this," "not with

9 WHAT IF WE PUT THE AUDIENCE FIRST?

kids," "save for later" would change the rails in ways you can feel. You'd get something as simple as a reviewable history—this is what we think you did, this is how we're using it—and the ability to say, "Ignore everything from last Saturday morning, that was my nephew," without starting from scratch. Agency isn't a settings menu on top of the product. It's the product being willing to show its work and let you correct it.

Identity has the same problem, just one level deeper. Profiles and Kids Mode were supposed to fix the "who's watching" question, but they treat identity as static. This is Dad's profile. This is Mom's profile. This is the kid's profile. In practice, that's not how viewing works. Dad on Tuesday night alone is not Dad on Saturday morning with a seven-year-old in the room. Mom on a plane with a tablet is not Mom half-asleep on the couch. A teenager doom-scrolling TikTok on their phone is not the same teenager half-present on the couch while something runs in the background.

The living room makes those contradictions obvious because it forces them to share a glass surface. The system can't tell who's in the room. It asks the same "Who's watching?" question every time and treats whatever answer it gets as if that person now exists in a vacuum.

If you start from the audience instead of the account, identity stops being a static label and becomes a shorthand for a situation. Alone or together. Background or focus. Short and light, or up for something new and demanding. Kids in the room or not. You don't need a twenty-question quiz to get there. Two or three honest prompts, or a decent first guess with a way to correct it, would get most households surprisingly far.

Once you admit those modes exist, they become useful elsewhere. A show doesn't have to be "for you" in every context. It can be tagged, explicitly or implicitly, as something that works when you're cooking, or when the whole family is watching, or when you're awake enough to read subtitles. A bad recommendation doesn't have to be a referendum on who you are as a viewer; it can simply be wrong for tonight. "Not for weeknights." "Save for vacation." "More like this when I'm watching alone."

The point isn't to turn the living room into a cockpit full of switches. It's the opposite. A little bit of honest modeling up front—this is who's here, this is what they're up for—shrinks the space of possible answers. The real work is forcing the conversation platforms currently dodge.

Trust is where older discovery systems still have the edge. We used to know where recommendations came from. You knew which friend loved slow art films and which one only watched superhero movies. You knew the critic whose reviews you always fought with, and the one whose taste tracked yours eerily well. You knew the clerk at the local video store was a horror obsessive and calibrated accordingly. The recommendation arrived with visible priors attached and part of the pleasure was learning them.

The modern home screen has almost none of that. Tiles appear as if handed down from nowhere: "Trending," "Because You Watched," "Top Picks For You." Behind those bland labels is a mix of licensing priorities, marketing campaigns, house quotas and, yes, real behavioral modeling. But the surface pretends to be neutral while everything underneath it is anything but. When it gets it wrong, you have nobody to argue with, and when it gets it right, you have nobody to thank. There is no relationship, just exposure.

Even people who build these home screens will tell you: what's labeled personalization is often just paid placement in a different font. Most home-screen "For You" rows are driven by commercial placement agreements, not viewer desire. Platforms use the language of identity—"Because you watched," "Top Picks For You"—to hide a shelf-rental business. It's not just misaligned with your needs. It's structurally dishonest about what the interface is doing. When a tile appears in your "personalized" feed, you have no way to know if it's there because the algorithm thinks you'll like it, or because someone paid to put it there. The opacity isn't a bug. It's the business model.

Audience-first discovery doesn't pretend to be neutral. It admits that all curation comes from somewhere and labels it honestly. Some rows are house picks. Some are driven by what people like you actually finished. Some come from human beings you chose to follow—friends, critics, curators. Some point outside the walls of the app. You don't have to agree with all of them. But you should be able to see which is which.

We already have sketches of what that feels like. Spotify's Discover Weekly and Release Radar work partly because they're bounded and rhythmic. You get a finite set of songs at a predictable time. You test them. You decide whether the list "gets" you this week. Over time, that becomes a relationship, even if it's with a model.

That's trust through cadence: a system that shows up on schedule and earns a weekly yes or no.

Letterboxd does something similar with movies by making taste transparent. You don't just see a score; you see who gave it and what else they've loved or hated. A four-star rating means something different from one person than from another, and the platform doesn't hide that. You're not being 'personalized'—you're following taste you can actually read.

Twitch is another useful tell. When a streamer "raids" another channel at the end of a show, they're doing old-fashioned lead-in programming with modern tools. You don't need a machine to explain why you're there. Someone you already trust took you there on purpose and told you so. The recommendation comes with a face, and the face is accountable.

Audience-first systems don't have to copy those mechanics directly, but they should steal the honesty. If a row exists because the platform needs to drive viewership to a particular show, say so. If it exists because a critic you chose to follow put it together, say that instead. Trust is a relationship. You can't bolt it onto the side of a black box. You have to show your work.

Here's what it looks like when the system doesn't put the audience first. At a recent streaming conference, during audience Q&A, a reporter stood up and told a story about a friend of his. The friend pays for all the right services—the big sports bundle, a couple of league apps, some general streamers. On paper, he's the ideal legal

9 WHAT IF WE PUT THE AUDIENCE FIRST? 143

customer. In practice, he hardly uses any of them to watch sports. Instead, he goes to a single illegal site that has every game, every league, in one place, with a clean interface. He's not doing it to save money; he's already paying. He does it because it's the only version of the product that treats his time like it's worth anything.

This isn't a sports-fan morality tale. It's a governance and infrastructure failure. Rights carve-outs, blackouts, and app silos create a user experience so bad that even a fully paying customer is nudged toward theft. And you can't fix it by putting all sports in one service—those rights fees are fragmented and overpaid for on purpose because they're tentpoles, and those checks to leagues and athletes assume multiple bidders and exclusivity. The missing piece isn't unified rights; it's infrastructure that sits above rights: a coherent, identity-aware layer that knows who you are, what you pay for, where the rights actually live tonight, and routes you to the legal stream with one click.

Right now, every rights-holder insists on being their own app, their own UX, their own identity island. No one with power is incentivized to build the neutral orchestration layer on top of that mess. So pirates do it instead. The thieves get the traffic. The leagues get stolen from—not because there's no willingness to pay, but because the "official" stack is so fragmented and hostile that the best-designed product in the ecosystem is the one that doesn't have a legal right to exist.

Intent is where the entire question turns. Platform-first discovery optimizes for "What will get you to click?" Audience-first discovery cares about "Why are you here?" Those sound like cousins, but they produce opposite products. The first leans toward surprise and compulsion; the second leans toward fit.

Right now, platforms treat intent as invisible. They make you express it indirectly through behavior—scrolling, hovering, bailing out ten minutes in—and fold that into "engagement." Apple's old Genius sidebar on iTunes was closer to the right question: it would ask whether you were in the mood for something new or something familiar and then actually obeyed the answer. We've somehow gone backward from there.

If you put the audience first, you'd ask a small version of that question at the beginning of a session. Alone or together. Lean back or lean in. Short, medium, or long. You'd take three answers seriously enough to shrink the universe, then go to work.

Once intent is on the table, everything else gets easier. Agency has something to attach to; you can say "not tonight" in a way that doesn't erase your preferences forever. Identity modes have a reason to exist; they're just structured shorthand for common intents you keep revisiting. Trust has a context; you can start to learn which sources are good at which jobs. Instead of a single monolithic "For You" feed, you start to get a set of interpretable lenses: for you in this room, in this mode, right now.

There are already small, everyday examples of intent-based curation hiding in the open. A critic's list of "comfort movies for rainy Sundays." A friend's email with "stuff that worked with my kids around seven." A community's running thread of "smart but not homework" recommendations. None of those are built into the TV. They live in group chats, newsletters, Discords, places where platforms mostly aren't looking. They work because they name the situation first and the taste second.

Bring all of this back to the couch, and the difference in posture becomes obvious. Platform-first discovery treats you as an exhaust trail of behavior to be captured and monetized. Audience-first discovery treats you as someone trying to get from a vague feeling—"we should watch something"—to a decent choice with minimal friction. The metric shifts from how many tiles you saw to how little work it took to land somewhere everyone in the room can live with.

We don't yet have a full-scale, room-first discovery layer running across TV and social. What we do have are early signals. A music service that made a finite, weekly playlist people trust enough to check on purpose. A film community that lets you follow actual human taste instead of demographic cohorts. Live platforms where one creator can still walk you into another's room and tell you why it matters. Self-selected communities that remain some of the most powerful recommendation engines on earth without a single line of "Because you watched…" copy.

None of them fixes the Friday night problem by themselves. Together, they outline a different contract. People aren't just data sources for an ad product; they're participants in the act of finding something that fits.

Up to now, we've been building the machine that makes content easier to ship and easier to consume. What comes next—the work of the rest of this part of the book—is the machine that makes connection easier to find. Channels built for return instead of one-off spikes. Systems that recognize who you are in different contexts instead of locking you into one profile forever. Environments where ritual and community do as much work as any row of thumbnails.

This chapter is the hinge between the room and the rebuild. It asks the question the current infrastructure keeps dodging: what if we put the audience first? The next three chapters are my attempt at an answer.

10 CHANNELS, NOT SHOWS_

THE FEED HAS WON, at least for now. We live in a world of infinite content, optimized for short bursts of attention and relentlessly organized by platforms that prioritize engagement over meaning. The result is a familiar exhaustion—endless scroll, decision fatigue, and a constant sense of being pulled forward without direction. The discovery problem we've been circling isn't just about viewer frustration, it's about the collapse of systems that once helped people find what mattered most.

If you start from the room instead of the catalog, you don't design a "better show." You design a lane that answers a recurring situation: after school, pre-dinner, late-night, Saturday morning. A place you can just put on and know the room will be fine. Channels, not shows.

And once you see it that way, the question shifts again: not just how we find content, but what we're actually looking for. What if the very unit of consumption we've been optimizing for—the individual "show" or "video"—is outdated in a world of infinite choice and fragmented attention?

When I was at Blip, one of our top creators was Doug Walker, better known as the Nostalgia Critic. He wasn't chasing viral hits or cranking out one-off episodes designed to spike traffic, he was building something more durable. His fans didn't just watch a video, they subscribed to him—his tone, his rhythm, his recurring segments, his critical lens on old media. There was a formula, yes, but it wasn't empty repetition, it was consistent identity that viewers could rely on.

He released new videos on a predictable cadence, spun off side projects, and collaborated with other creators in the same orbit. Over time, what he was really doing wasn't running a "show" in the traditional sense, it was running a channel—not in the YouTube technical sense, but in the emotional one, a destination, a voice, a trusted filter.

What made it work wasn't scale or production value, it was trust. Fans didn't just consume his content, they relied on it, and that reliability, more than any algorithmic advantage, kept them coming back.

That logic matters even more now that YouTube—born on phones and laptops—is the most-watched app on living-room TVs. The habits that made sense on personal screens are now playing out on the shared one. When the same feeds land on the biggest screen in the house, the job changes: people don't want a single episode, they want a dependable channel.

This is the essence of the shift we're living through, from shows to channels, a reimagining of how content is organized, discovered, and consumed—away from the ephemeral, feed-based logic of trending clips and toward curated destinations built around shared passions, niche identities, and deeper forms of belonging. It's the foundation for a post-feed video experience, and we've seen it before.

There are obstacles baked into today's platforms. The Subscriptions tab exists, but it's buried and deprioritized. Session time grows when the platform chooses what's next. Tools that help channels—community posts, memberships, channel pages—sit behind the feed's primary logic. And there's the economics, too: channels need a baseline of production and a stable cadence to be legible, but the feed rewards spikes and novelty. Direct habits risk becoming creator loyalty, which is exactly what platforms try to keep for themselves. Most attempts fail because one of those collapses.

For most of the last century, "shows" were the atomic unit of entertainment. From radio dramas to television sitcoms, a "show" was a self-contained narrative—a specific program with a beginning, middle, and end, produced by a studio and broadcast at a scheduled time. Even in the early days of streaming, Netflix, HBO, and Amazon continued this paradigm, simply moving "shows" from a linear schedule to an on-demand library, with the focus remaining on the singular piece of content, the individual title.

But this model is breaking down. In a world where millions of videos are uploaded every day, the individual "show" struggles to gain and maintain relevance. A single "show," however brilliant, exists in a vacuum—its discoverability relies heavily on external factors like platform algorithms, trending lists, or aggressive marketing campaigns, and without a broader framework, it's competing against millions of other pieces for the same fleeting attention.

Once you finish a "show," what then? The platform immediately pushes you to another, often unrelated, "show," and there's no inherent loyalty beyond the single narrative—engagement is fleeting, tied to the conclusion of a story rather than the continuation of a relationship. Imagine trying to keep up with every new "show" released across all streaming services—it's an impossible task, and the sheer volume overwhelms, leading to the paralysis we discussed. The "show" was designed for scarcity, not superabundance.

The problem with the "show" mentality is that it assumes attention is a finite resource to be captured and then released—you watch this show, then that show—but what if interest doesn't work like that? What if viewers want to stay within a stream of content that consistently satisfies a deeper, ongoing curiosity or passion, rather than constantly jumping from one discrete narrative to the next?

The concept of "channels" re-emerges here, but radically redefined for the digital age. These aren't the numbered, linear broadcast channels of old, they're thematic, curated streams of content built around passion and identity, designed to provide a continuous, lean-back experience for a specific, engaged audience. On a phone, that might look like a single creator's tightly defined area of expertise. On the TV, it starts to look like a place everyone can sit in without flinching.

This shift isn't theoretical, it's already visible in how

people organize and engage with content today. Instead of a generic "Comedy" section, imagine a "channel" dedicated solely to "Dry British Panel Shows," "Surreal Animated Shorts for Adults," or "Stand-Up Comedy from the 1970s"—these aren't just playlists but living, evolving collections, often with new content added regularly, curated by an expert or a community. Instead of a single video about building a miniature train set, imagine a "channel" that takes you on a journey through the history of model railroading, different techniques, product reviews, and interviews with master builders, where the content builds on itself, offering a continuous learning or entertainment experience. Viewers no longer passively receive content served by an algorithm guessing what they'll click, instead, they enter a channel because it aligns with a specific, enduring interest, pulling themselves in rather than being pushed.

These new digital channels share several characteristics. Every piece of content within the channel—every video, every live stream—is deeply aligned with a specific subject, mood, or identity, not just about genre but a highly specific, often niche focus that resonates with a dedicated audience. The "channel operator," whether an individual creator, a small team, or a community, acts as a trusted filter, and their value isn't just in creating content but in discerningly selecting, organizing, and often contextualizing relevant material from across the internet, or producing original content perfectly tailored to the channel's theme.

While still on demand, these channels offer a lean-back experience—relaxed, continuous viewing without the constant 'what next?' work. It feels less like work and more like a comfortable, ongoing conversation. Viewers don't just consume content, they inhabit an identity by participating in the channel—being "a subscriber to the 'Vintage Sci-Fi Film Commentary' channel" means something more than simply "watching a lot of sci-fi," it implies a shared passion, a specific taste, and often, a community of like-minded individuals. The connection is with the channel operator, the curator who consistently provides value within that specific thematic space, building loyalty and trust far beyond any single piece of content.

In practice, the most resilient versions of these channels rarely belong to a single face. They work more like a good neighborhood mall: an anchor tenant you recognize, surrounded by a rotating roster of complementary shops. A flagship creator can set the tone, but the channel itself is the promise. If one contributor burns out, disappears, or needs to step back, the lane still holds. From the couch, no one says, "Put on [Creator Name]." They say, "Put on the home channel," or "Put on the gaming channel." They're asking for a reliable mood the whole room can sit inside, not a single personality.

The shift isn't about re-creating cable TV, it's about taking the best elements of purposeful curation and community-building and applying them to the unbounded potential of the internet, organizing the vast, disorganized library into spaces where people actually want to spend time, each dedicated to a specific subject and guided by someone who genuinely cares.

The algorithmic black box, as discussed, is failing us because it optimizes for engagement, not for relevance or genuine discovery—and the "channels, not shows" model works because it returns to the oldest discovery system we have: human curation, the thing the feed keeps pretending it replaced.

In the digital age, this role has been eroded by the sheer volume of content and the rise of automated systems, but in a world of infinite noise, the most valuable commodity is a trusted filter. A good human curator doesn't just show you what's popular, they show you what's resonant, understanding nuance, context, and the subtle shifts in human taste that algorithms cannot grasp.

TikTok's For You Page fails the curation test despite sophisticated algorithmic targeting. The platform optimizes for immediate engagement over sustained trust-building—a creator might go viral with dance content one day and cooking tips the next, fracturing any coherent curatorial voice. The algorithm serves the feed, not the relationship.

A "channel" in this new paradigm could be run by a dedicated individual, a small team, or even a decentralized community. Imagine a historian who curates a "channel" on forgotten aspects of the Cold War—they don't just upload documentaries but provide commentary, source materials, interviews, and even host live discussions, with their value coming from deep expertise and a discerning eye. A team passionate about sustainability might create a "channel" that aggregates the best documentaries, explainer videos, and citizen journalism on climate solutions, interspersed with their own original content and interviews with innovators, creating a cohesive narrative around a critical global issue. A highly engaged fan community for a niche video game might collectively curate a "channel" of speedruns, lore discussions, fan animations, and historical gameplay footage, often with live commentary and group watch parties, where the trust comes from shared passion and collective expertise.

The currency of these channels is reliability, not views—it's the belief that when you tune into a "channel," you will consistently receive high-quality, relevant content that aligns with your specific interest. Trust is earned through consistent curation, a clear editorial voice, and a deep understanding of the audience's needs, which is the opposite of the algorithm's opaque, constantly shifting logic. It's the human algorithm, built on shared passion and mutual respect.

The "feed" has conditioned us for constant engagement, demanding active participation through swiping, clicking, liking, commenting, and sharing. It's a relentless treadmill built to maximize the time we spend on the platform, and while it works for quick bursts of entertainment or information, it's exhausting for sustained consumption.

The "channels, not shows" model restores a more lean-back, purposeful viewing experience. Once you've chosen a channel, the cognitive load drops—there's no need to scroll or deliberate because the content flows, with each piece falling within your chosen interest, like tuning into a curated radio station where every song matches your taste and mood. Thematic cohesion lets viewers fully settle into a subject without being pulled between disparate topics, allowing a sense of flow that supports deeper focus and engagement without interruptions from unrelated recommendations.

You enter a "channel" with a specific purpose—to learn about space exploration, unwind with ambient music videos, or explore experimental animation—and this intentionality turns consumption from accidental discovery into purposeful engagement, about choosing your destination rather than letting the current carry you. Over time, these channels develop a familiar rhythm through consistent voice, predictable quality, and deep focus on a beloved subject, all contributing to a sense of comfort and belonging that builds a lasting relationship between viewer and channel, creating a sense of "home" in the digital chaos. At its best, that's what a good lane feels like on the living-room TV: you can just put it on and the room will be fine.

This isn't about replacing all short-form, attention-grabbing content—it's about offering an alternative, a refuge from the endless scroll, for moments when viewers want deeper engagement, sustained learning, or a more relaxed, curated experience. It's the digital equivalent of settling into a comfortable armchair with a well-chosen book, rather than frantically flipping through channels in a crowded bar.

For creators, adopting the "channels, not shows" model requires a strategic shift—from chasing viral one-offs to building sustainable, purpose-driven ecosystems—and it's a blueprint for longevity, genuine audience ownership, and renewed creative control.

The first step is defining your niche with precision, avoiding vague labels like "comedy creator" or "gamer" and instead pinpointing a specific, passionate intersection of interests—"I curate underrated documentaries about overlooked historical figures" or "I explore the philosophical implications of artificial intelligence through short animated essays"—because the sharper the niche, the stronger the signal to your audience.

Increasingly, your value will come from filtering, organizing, and contextualizing content, not only from producing it. This can include aggregating external content, collaborating with other creators, and producing tailored original content that fills gaps in the curated narrative, with the goal being to build a body of work that flows naturally from one piece to the next, instead of chasing fleeting trends. Every piece should serve the channel's larger narrative and purpose, strengthening loyalty and increasing watch time within your ecosystem.

This stands in sharp contrast to platforms like TikTok, where the creator experience is shaped by perpetual trend-chasing. The pressure to slot content into the latest audio snippet, meme format, or challenge often rewards reactive participation over sustained authorship, and while these formats can generate reach, they rarely build identity or loyalty. What's missing is a throughline, and channels solve for that, replacing momentary alignment with cumulative authority.

You don't need a rigid schedule like linear TV, but establishing a rhythm for your channel—a weekly deep dive, a monthly curated compilation, a daily news roundup within your niche—builds anticipation and creates viewing rituals for your audience. As we've seen already, scale without structure is a trap, and for these channels, it means direct communication channels, diversified monetization, and modular content production. Treat your channel as a hub for like-minded people—engage directly, spark conversations, and create spaces where members connect with one another, not just with you—shifting viewers from passive consumers to active participants and building a resilient, invested audience.

The focus shifts from individual pieces of content as the product to the channel itself, moving away from the fleeting nature of virality toward the lasting value of thematic depth and curated trust. It's the evolution from content producer to media architect.

While the phrase "channels, not shows" may be new, the principles behind it are already shaping some of the most effective media strategies online, and these examples show what that future looks like in practice.

Consider Kurzgesagt, In a Nutshell (science explainers), Noclip (video game documentaries), or Art History with James Payne—these aren't just collections of unrelated videos, they operate as thematic channels. Their content is consistently high-quality, closely aligned with a specific intellectual curiosity, and their audience expects a certain caliber of deep dive, building loyalty by delivering a distinct type of knowledge or experience, not just chasing viral hits. Viewers don't just watch a Kurzgesagt video, they follow the channel because it reliably feeds their desire for complex science made accessible.

The most sophisticated YouTube creators are already treating channels as arbitrage instruments. They're stitching their back catalogs into 24/7 feeds, calling them FAST channels, and tapping into CTV (connected Television) CPMs that can run an order of magnitude higher than what they see on mobile. The distinction between "premium TV" and "user-generated content" is a billing construct, not a structural one. When MrBeast-level creators can repackage their YouTube output as a linear channel and command TV advertising rates, it's proof that channelization is the natural form in saturation—and that the lines separating platforms, formats, and economic tiers are thinner than the decks pretend.

Many successful podcasts function as "channels" rather than just individual "shows"—shows like Radiolab or Serial built loyal audiences by consistently delivering on a specific thematic promise, and networks like Radiotopia or Earwolf also demonstrate this principle, curating collections of shows that share editorial coherence. Listeners don't just pick one episode, they subscribe to feeds knowing they will reliably serve their particular intellectual curiosity.

While often created by traditional media companies, the rise of services like Pluto TV or Tubi's themed channels—dedicated to classic TV series or genres like action movies and true crime—shows clear demand for lean-back, curated streams. These mimic linear TV, but succeed by offering highly specific, predictable programming that removes decision fatigue, and for creators, the lesson isn't necessarily to join these platforms. Some are building their own.

As we saw earlier, Discord servers and niche online communities are already powerful discovery engines, and they also function as proto-channels. A Discord server dedicated to "Sustainable Urban Farming" might feature threads for techniques, resource sharing, tool reviews, and even local meetups, where the "content" is the collective knowledge and shared passion of the members.

While text-based, Substack shows how the "channel" model works in practice—subscribing to a newsletter means committing to a steady stream of insights, analysis, or creative work from a specific, trusted voice. You're not reading one article, you're entering an ongoing conversation within a defined intellectual or creative space.

These examples, in their diverse forms, point to the same underlying truth—people want curated, thematic experiences that match their passions, not endless, undifferentiated content. They want a guide, a filter, and a steady stream of what they love, not a firehose of everything.

But while the logic of channels is intuitive and increasingly visible across formats, it can still feel abstract, so what does this shift look like in practice? What does it take to build a modern creator channel? One of the clearest examples is hiding in plain sight.

Perhaps no creator better exemplifies the shift from "shows" to "channels" than Andrew Rea, better known as Babish. When he uploaded his first cooking video in 2016, recreating the Parks and Recreation burger cook-off, he wasn't trying to build a channel—he was making a show, or more precisely, a shtick that combined cinematic cooking with fanboy pop culture.

Over time, something shifted as Binging with Babish became the foundation, not the format. Rea didn't just lean into the demand for food-meets-fandom, he built an ecosystem around it—Basics with Babish taught fundamentals in a stripped-down, practical style, Stump Sohla brought in guest talent and co-branded voice, and eventually, it all evolved into the Babish Culinary Universe, a modular, multi-format creator channel with recurring IP, guest hosts, and a consistent editorial identity.

What makes Babish instructive isn't subscriber count or longevity, it's the channel logic behind the success. He didn't chase the feed, he built a viewing environment where viewers knew what they were getting—visual consistency, dry humor, voiceover-forward presentation, and comfort-meets-creativity—and even as formats diversified, the identity stayed coherent. New shows didn't compete with the original, they expanded the surface area without diluting the core signal.

The structure enabled more than content rhythm, it enabled repeatable monetization. Babish launched cookbooks, high-end kitchen gear, and merch lines not just from personality appeal but from a recognizable brand environment, and as more creators entered the food space with flashier production or algorithm-chasing trends, Babish thrived by staying anchored in modular design and predictable cadence.

His path marks a larger shift in the creator economy—away from treating each video like a standalone product, and toward building networks of recurring context. Babish didn't build a viral hit, he built a viewing habit, and the distinction matters. In a feed-first world, attention is transient, but a well-designed channel creates its own gravity, and Babish showed you don't need to chase the algorithm when you design a system the algorithm wants to serve.

The rise of "channels, not shows" is a counter-movement—reorienting media toward intentional connection that serves specific, deeply held passions and builds enduring relationships grounded in trust and shared identity. True value in the digital age isn't about reach, it's about resonance.

Individual shows won't disappear—blockbusters and episodic narratives will remain—but the dominant mode of consumption and discovery will shift. Just as television evolved from a handful of broadcast channels to a vast cable universe, then to on-demand streaming, internet video is poised for its next major evolution.

The shift has implications for every player in the ecosystem. For platforms, it means moving from pure algorithmic optimization toward enabling creator-led curation and fostering deeper, more specialized communities. For advertisers, it's about alignment with specific passions and highly engaged niche communities. For viewers, it means escaping decision fatigue and returning to joyful discovery. For creators, it's a path to sustainable livelihoods, true audience ownership, and deep niche passions.

The solution to the discovery crisis, and the blueprint for the next phase of the creator economy, won't come from perfecting the old factory model of generic content and algorithmic push. It lies in recognizing the human desire for purpose, curation, and belonging, building new signals that point not to the loudest noise but to the most resonant connection. These signals are the channels, built by passionate creators for dedicated communities.

11 IDENTITY OVER INTERFACE_

ALGORITHMS CAN'T TELL who's watching—only what was watched. A kid's cartoon ruins your Netflix recommendations for weeks, "Because You Watched" rows feel like spam. The system matches content to behavior, but behavior is contextual. You're not one user; you're a parent at 7 a.m., a solo viewer at 11 p.m., a co-watcher on Friday night. Identity, not interface, is the missing variable.

This helps explain why discovery keeps failing, even as the catalogs keep growing. Platforms optimize for content matching—genre, actor, runtime. But what we need is context matching: who's watching, when, with whom, and why. When systems recognize identity states instead of static profiles, discovery stops guessing and starts working.

The modern streaming landscape is overflowing with content, yet discovery feels more elusive than ever. We're flooded with "recommendations" but still feel unseen, unheard, unserved. For all their computational power, algorithms falter the moment human nuance enters the frame. They can track what was selected, what played, and how long it streamed. They can't tell if anyone was truly watching—or whether it was you, someone else, or a group together.

Consider the shared family account: one profile for the entire household, the main screen everyone uses for entertainment. One night you watch a gritty prestige drama that's the talk of the office. The next morning, your teenager logs in to a home screen suddenly overtaken by Scandinavian crime thrillers. Or you spend a weekend watching animated classics with your young son, only to find your "For You" section now a saccharine parade of talking animals—ignoring that you're an adult seeking intellectual stimulation, not cartoons. Algorithms assume a static, singular identity for each profile, blind to the fluid, contextual, and often contradictory nature of human preference. They're optimized for content, not for the person.

Programmers have always understood the messiness underneath, even when the decks pretended otherwise. ABC Family built its schedule "for millennial moms" and then quietly rode the fact that twelve- and fourteen-year-old girls were the ones glued to the screen. Streaming grids do the same thing now: the official demo is 25–45, but the aspirational 14–25s are sitting right there on the couch or watching the same shows later on their phones. A smarter system would stop pretending there's a single, stable end user and treat the household itself as the unit of design—a shifting cluster of overlapping identities, not one heroic profile.

Knowing who is watching—and in what mode—either

requires explicit selection (adds friction and reduces engagement) or inference (raises privacy risk and liability). Platforms already struggle with basic age accuracy; adding mood, intent, and co-viewing raises risk without obvious upside. Context-aware systems are also harder and pricier to run than content matching: real-time context, multi-profile identity, session-aware personalization. The revenue case is murky. Will it lift session time? Reduce churn meaningfully? Unlock a new line of business? Cheaper wins—faster loads, stickier notifications, better trend-matching—are safer bets.

Disney learned this the expensive way in 2025. The FTC fined them $10 million for COPPA (Children's Online Privacy Protection Act) violations—not because they couldn't tell what was kids' content, but because they chose not to label it that way. On Disney's YouTube channels, videos built for under-13 audiences were left off as "Made for Kids," letting YouTube collect data and serve targeted ads anyway. YouTube had flagged the issue years earlier, but Disney stuck with channel-level defaults that privileged frictionless publishing over identity accuracy. The settlement forced a compliance program and stricter kids-labeling gates, but the underlying issue remains: platforms prioritize growth-friendly defaults over precision because the metrics reward speed, not correctness.

There's a control issue, too. Identity modes—Professional, Parent, Unwinder—return agency to the user. Respecting those boundaries can reduce total time. Today's systems optimize across all contexts; more intentional use may be better for people and worse for the primary metric. Platforms optimize for engagement and ad impressions, not for user satisfaction or creator sustainability. If identity-first doesn't clearly improve those metrics, it stalls. Which is why better discovery keeps emerging off-platform—in taste networks, newsletters, and communities—rather than inside the feeds.

This is the core limitation of today's content-matching systems: they operate at the surface, fixating on what's playing—the genre, the cast, the runtime, the clicks and skips—while ignoring the layered question of who is watching. Matching content is easy; understanding the viewer is hard, and that's the part that matters now.

Most platforms are still built around interfaces: the home screen, the search bar, the infinite scroll, the "Up Next" queue, the category grid. All presume the user is a browser—wandering digital shelves, deciding what to watch, read, or buy.

But that's not how people navigate anymore, especially younger audiences.

They're not browsing; they're expressing—not searching for content but searching for themselves, reflected in a voice, a moment, a micro-genre. This identity-seeking behavior is visible across platforms. Many now function as curated identity feeds, where users build a public-facing version of who they are—or who they want to be. Content isn't just consumed; it's selected, filtered, and arranged to project a sense of self. What you save, post, or even linger on becomes part of that image. For recommendation systems, this ambient curation offers profound insight, if they're willing to look beyond the obvious.

11 IDENTITY OVER INTERFACE

The shift is clear: from interface-driven consumption to identity-driven connection. But to understand why it matters, we need to see what it's replacing.

For decades, content matching was simple: broad categories and explicit preferences. You liked action movies, you got more action movies. You bought a rock album, you got more rock albums. The digital age layered in behavioral data—if you watched one show, and people who watched it also tended to watch another, the system recommended that next. Statistical correlation became the bedrock of recommendation engines.

But correlation isn't causation, and past behavior doesn't always predict future desire, especially without context. The flaw is an over-reliance on IP-centric matching. You watch a documentary on space exploration and suddenly you're inundated with every documentary on every topic—the algorithm sees "documentary" (a what) but misses "fascination with the cosmos and scientific discovery" (a who). You enjoy a specific actor in a comedy, so the system recommends all their other works, even if they're in a drama or niche indie film far from your broader taste. It's matching a what (the performer) without understanding who you are when you engage with that performer. Algorithms excel at serving more of what you've already consumed or what's similar to it, reinforcing existing preferences but rarely surfacing something that speaks to an unarticulated desire. If you watch true crime often, the system assumes that's the only version of you, missing the nuance of mood, company, or fleeting curiosity.

But you're not—you're different when you're alone

versus with your kids, different on a Tuesday morning than on a Saturday night. You are not one user; you are many, and until the system understands that, it will keep showing you the wrong version of yourself.

True personalization doesn't begin with content; it begins with the person. It recognizes that identity in media consumption is fluid, contextual, and deeply personal. It's about unpacking the layers of "who is watching" beyond a demographic profile.

Think about a moment of genuine discovery: you're scrolling aimlessly, feeling a vague sense of unease. Not sad, not angry, just... unsettled. A friend messages: "Hey, I just watched this short film. It's weird, but it made me feel seen." You click the link, and for twenty minutes you're transported. The film doesn't solve your problems, but it perfectly captures an emotion you couldn't name. You didn't search for "weird film that makes me feel seen." The algorithm couldn't have found it. Your friend understood a subtle, unarticulated emotional need, a part of your who, and made a recommendation that resonated.

This is the power of understanding the nuance of "who."

We inhabit different "identities" throughout the day, and our content needs shift with them. The Professional looks for deep dives, analytical content, industry insights, while the Parent seeks calming, educational, or entertaining content for children. The Hobbyist pursues highly specific tutorials, reviews, or discussions tied to a niche passion. The Unwinder wants lighthearted entertainment, escapism, or soothing background experiences, and the

11 IDENTITY OVER INTERFACE

Socializer finds content to share, discuss, or co-experience with others.

Creators understand this instinctively, even when platforms don't. In 2024, beauty creators started launching LinkedIn channels—not because LinkedIn's algorithm recommended it, but because they recognized the platform demanded a different identity performance. The same creator who does full-glam tutorials on Instagram and TikTok adapts to "professional mode" on LinkedIn: career advice for makeup artists, business strategy for beauty entrepreneurs, industry analysis framed through a corporate lens. Same person, same expertise, completely different contextual identity. The content shifts to match how users see themselves on that platform. LinkedIn's audience isn't browsing for makeup tips—they're in Professional mode, seeking career value. Smart creators don't fight that context; they inhabit it.

Our internal state dictates what we seek. Sometimes we want to be challenged, other times comforted. We might crave intellectual stimulation, or simply a mindless escape. An algorithm that only tracks genre preferences can't detect the subtle shifts between seeking solace, seeking excitement, or seeking creative inspiration. Imagine an interface that allowed you to filter content not by genre, but by mood: "Something to make me laugh," "Something to make me think," "Something to help me relax and fall asleep."

The people we're with change our viewing habits. The living room TV, a traditionally communal device, often struggles with individual personalization. A single user profile is a poor fit for a family of four with diverse ages and tastes. We often resort to lowest-common-denominator content or endless negotiation because the system doesn't account for the collective "who" currently engaging with the screen.

A recommendation system that only knows you like "comedies" will fail to distinguish between a stand-up special you'd watch alone to decompress and a family-friendly sitcom you'd watch with your kids. The algorithm doesn't know which version of you is currently engaging with the screen.

Our choice of device often signals our intent. Watching a short, punchy news summary on your phone during a commute is different from watching a feature-length documentary on your smart TV after dinner. The mobile device often implies quick consumption, utility, or bite-sized entertainment, while the TV might indicate a deeper, more immersive experience. Current algorithms track device usage but often fail to translate it into a deeper understanding of the user's identity in that specific moment.

Your audience isn't a monolith; they have shifting needs and different intentions depending on when and why they show up. Are you serving the "who" or just the "what"? The platforms, by focusing on the "what" and the aggregated "watch time," are missing the richer, more human signals that drive genuine engagement and satisfaction.

The solution to understanding the "who" doesn't necessarily lie in asking users more questions or forcing them to manually update their profiles. It lies in building systems that can infer context and intent from subtle, implicit signals, much like a good human curator.

The limitations of stated preferences are clear. People often claim to like "thought-provoking dramas" but spend hours watching reality TV. Their explicit preferences, driven by aspiration or social signaling, don't always align with their actual behavior in a relaxed, private setting. Survey-based recommendation systems will always fall short.

Instead, we need to tap into implicit signals. Watching a specific type of content consistently at 7 a.m. on weekdays suggests a morning routine, perhaps for news or a commute podcast, while watching a different type of content late on a Saturday night suggests leisure, relaxation, or social viewing. These patterns are powerful indicators of contextual identity.

The choice of device can signal intent and the "version of you" engaging: a mobile device for quick news updates, a tablet for reading long-form articles in bed, a smart TV for family movie night, a computer for a deep-dive tutorial. If a user only watches children's cartoons when their profile is logged in simultaneously with a child's profile, the system should infer that these views are context-dependent and not a shift in the primary adult's long-term taste. Group profiles, like the ones Netflix introduced belatedly, are a step in this direction, but true communal understanding goes deeper.

A user might search for "action movie" but consistently watch only the first 10 minutes before switching—the algorithm should learn from the actual consumption behavior rather than just the initial search query, indicating a potential mismatch in intent or quality expectation. Not just if a user watches, but how they watch: do they finish the video? Do they rewind? Do they pause frequently? Do they interact with comments or share the content? This depth of engagement is a stronger signal of resonance than mere click-through rates. A short viral clip that gets millions of fleeting partial views might be less valuable to the user's deeper satisfaction than a niche, hour-long documentary watched intently from start to finish by a smaller, dedicated audience.

This requires a shift from pure engagement metrics to "satisfaction" or "meaning" metrics. It's about designing algorithms that optimize for resonance rather than just retention. These seemingly insignificant data points become meaningful when combined and interpreted through a human lens, revealing a deeper truth about user identity and intent.

The challenge is immense. It requires more sophisticated AI that can identify patterns and infer meaning and context. It demands a willingness from platforms to move beyond the easy metric of "attention at all costs" and invest in a more nuanced understanding of their users.

For all the talk of individualized screens and hyper-personalization, much of our media consumption still happens on communal devices, especially the living-room TV. This shared screen presents a unique challenge to algorithms designed for a single user—and an immense opportunity for systems that understand the "collective who."

Think of the family that shares a streaming account. Dad wants a sports documentary, Mom wants a period

11 IDENTITY OVER INTERFACE

drama, and the kids want the latest animated film. The current system forces profile switching or a frustrating compromise. The algorithm, observing this chaotic activity, struggles to build a coherent profile for any individual, let alone the group.

The future of content matching must acknowledge—and design for—the shift from individual screens to communal hubs. The living-room TV isn't just a bigger monitor; it's a social and cultural anchor, a point of shared identity.

Designing for shared intent means making it effortless to switch between "Parent Mode," "Teen Mode," "Family Mode," etc., with associated algorithmic adjustments—not just about privacy but about context. It means allowing guests to watch without polluting the main user's recommendation engine, or offering curated "guest channels" for temporary use. Instead of just recommending individual shows, systems could suggest themed "Family Movie Nights" or "Friends' Game Night" channels that pull content suitable for a mixed audience, potentially from different services.

Platforms already hint at this communal identity layering—Close Friends Stories create intimate viewing circles, while separate accounts allow users to maintain different versions of themselves. The platform recognizes that identity shifts based on audience, even if it hasn't fully optimized for true co-viewing experiences. Features that allow multiple viewers to interact with the content, share reactions, or even vote on the next show create a more dynamic communal experience, moving beyond passive co-viewing to active co-engagement. A good TV lane doesn't just ask "Who is this for?" once; it quietly asks, every minute, "Who can sit in this without flinching?"

If your product only serves the individual, you're missing the village. The most successful platforms in the next era will be those that gracefully navigate the transition between individual and communal identities, understanding that the "who" can be singular or collective, and adapting their offerings accordingly.

The synthesis of "identity over interface" ties directly into the "channels, not shows" model from the previous chapter. It's the human element making sense of the data, orchestrating the signals into resonant connections. This isn't just about better algorithms; it's about a different philosophy of content matching—one driven by understanding the person first and the content second.

New signals for matching will emerge, prioritizing user intent and context. Instead of "I like dramas," the system understands, "I want something to relax to after a stressful day that doesn't require too much thought," or "I need content that helps me learn a new skill during my lunch break"—moving beyond static preferences to dynamic needs. Imagine content discovery where you select a mood ("calm," "energized," "thought-provoking," "silly") and the interface surfaces content tailored to that emotional state, regardless of genre, potentially involving visual cues, color palettes, or even ambient soundscapes that shift with the selected mood.

Beyond algorithmic suggestions, users could see what specific trusted communities or sub-groups are recommending for particular purposes: "What are the best long-form documentaries for focus, according to the 'Deep

Work' community I follow?" This leverages human trust and shared identity as a filter. Building on the "channels" concept, imagine deeply curated streams tailored to specific contextual identities: "The WFH Background Music Channel," "The Dinner Prep Entertainment Channel," "The Sunday Morning Think Piece Channel"—not just playlists but living, evolving, and often human-curated streams of content designed for a specific mode of being.

I saw this firsthand during my time as COO of Unreel, a streaming platform focused on AVOD (ad-supported video on demand) and linear channels. We powered over 200 creator-driven channels for partners like Studio71, Chicken Soup for the Soul, and others before being acquired by Bitcentral. The channels that performed best weren't built around individual influencers—they were thematic. One of the most effective was a Minecraft- and Roblox-themed gaming channel featuring creators like ThinkNoodles. Instead of anchoring everything around a single personality, we curated a network of creators aligned around a shared genre and audience vibe. Viewers weren't coming for a person; they were coming for the world—for the comfort, continuity, and collective identity the channel offered. It wasn't about following a face. It was about belonging to a space.

The role of creators in this new paradigm will be pivotal. Creators who understand their audience's "who" will build more resonant channels. They become curators of identity-specific experiences, crafting content not just for a broad demographic but for specific, nuanced versions of their audience. An ASMR creator might not just create relaxing sounds; they might curate specific "sleep channels" or "focus channels" that align with distinct identity states. An educator might offer "beginner learning channels" versus "advanced mastery channels." This requires deep empathy and a commitment to serving the user's true needs rather than just chasing viral trends.

The most impactful content experiences will be those that seamlessly align with our shifting identities and deeper human needs, not just our past clicks.

The shift from "shows" to "channels" is just one piece of a larger puzzle that redefines how we connect with media. The master key to solving the discovery problem and unlocking the next phase of the creator economy lies in recognizing that true personalization isn't about collecting more data points on what we watch. It's about developing a deep understanding of who we are when we watch it—our contextual identities, emotional states, social settings, and evolving intentions.

The future of content will be shaped by those who master the art of discerning the many "whos" that exist within each user. It will be built by creators, curators, and platforms that prioritize resonance over retention, meaning over watch time. This deeper understanding of human identity will enable experiences that are not just engaging but deeply satisfying, leading to genuine connection and a return to the purposeful discovery we often yearn for in our digital lives.

This shift has massive implications not just for creators, but for platforms, publishers, and advertisers. If identity is the primary filter, the old tools of discovery—genre, title, episode, search—start to lose relevance. People don't look for "documentary short films" or "sports analysis." They look for signals that match how they see themselves.

That's why the next generation of media won't be organized around content types. It will be organized around personality clusters—communities of identity. This doesn't mean we stop needing infrastructure; it means the infrastructure needs to flex. Platforms that keep forcing users into transactional, search-based navigation will lose out to those that understand identity first—systems that help users find what matches who they are, not just what they want.

It also means creators must understand that content is only half of their product. The other half is how people feel when they encounter it, how they relate to it, and what it helps them express about themselves. That's why community matters—not as a buzzword, but as a structural advantage. The creators who build lasting relationships won't be the ones who post the most; they'll be the ones who create places, not just posts—places where fans feel seen and connected, where showing up isn't just consumption but participation.

We're already seeing this with private Discords, paid newsletters, drop-in Zooms, and membership tiers. Not because creators are trying to monetize intimacy, but because intimacy is the new scarcity. Platforms will try to productize this—they'll build new features like badges, bonuses, chats, tiers—but the real movement will happen where identity is prioritized over interface, where people come for the connection, not just the content.

This changes how we think about monetization, growth, and brand partnerships—it reorients the whole system. In the feed era, attention was king; now affiliation matters more. You don't just want people to see your content; you want them to see themselves in it—and when people feel reflected, they stick around and start to belong.

This re-centering of the human element sets the stage for the next crucial signal: the human desire for shared meaning, connection, and belonging.

12 RITUAL & RETURN_

INFINITE CONTENT MAKES CONSISTENCY RARE, and ritual isn't a constraint—it's how people find their way back. A Tuesday drop is a promise, a room at 7 p.m. is gravity. For anyone trying to make a living in this ecosystem, it's also the only way the lane can keep the lights on.

If you think back to that Friday-night stalemate on the couch—the remote drifting from app to app while nothing quite lands—the thing everyone is really reaching for isn't a specific title. It's a place you can just put on and trust the room will be fine. Ritual is what turns that vague reach into something concrete.

Before the feeds, TV happened at a time. You didn't just choose what to watch, you chose when. That "when" created anticipation and a shared moment. Digital convenience killed the schedule and taught everyone to expect everything, anytime, anywhere. What it couldn't replace was the need for a place and a rhythm. We traded visible gates for invisible ones. The old schedule told you when; the new gate decides what starts without asking. And who shaped those gates? Not the platforms' story about choice but the users who stayed longest.

The platforms told a story about endless choice and personal control. The usage told a different one. Kids set the pattern first. Not because they have money, but because they have hours. The number that actually tilts these systems isn't headcount, it's time spent. The audience that stayed longest set the habits the rest now follow.

At Maker, you could see it if you looked under the surface—the visible slice was teens and young adults with loud comment threads, but under that was the mass that drove watch time: kids, including under-13. At the time, YouTube knew what was happening, but the fiction of an all-18+ audience was the easier posture. YouTube Kids existed for preschool and early elementary. The main site carried the culture. Admitting the obvious would have meant confronting COPPA at scale, retargeting, rebuilding yield, and telling the market the user story was more complicated than a clean deck. So everybody let the fiction stand and optimized around it. Penalties are a press cycle; defaults are forever. If the default routes kids through engagement systems, the fine isn't the cost—the habit is.

That pretense created a design blind spot. You can't build features for users you can't officially see, so YouTube built for the demo they could defend and let the actual audience—the one driving the hours—live in the gaps. The kids got interfaces designed for adults. The adults got ad yields subsidized by children. And everyone got to pretend the platform's biggest engagement driver was over eighteen and clicking of their own accord.

If you can't officially see the users who define your

patterns, you can't study their rituals or build for them. Interfaces stayed adult-facing—rows, reels, retention curves—while the durable signals of return were forming elsewhere: shared language, predictable cadence, people present together. The machine rewards starts; returns barely register, and when returns do register they're treated as a by-product instead of the point. YouTube wants Sesame Street not because it needs the revenue—it needs the reputation, a civic halo, legacy trust wrapping a commercial architecture still running on engagement and autoplay. Sesame Street teaches structure, YouTube teaches stickiness, and the second one wins because it controls what plays next.

If ritual is valuable, it's worth asking why feeds haven't already converged on it.

Feed and ritual run on different logics. Feeds optimize for starts—new sessions, new videos, new users. Ritual optimizes for returns—same users, same time, same place. Platforms instrument the first exquisitely and the second barely, and "returning viewer" doesn't separate stumble-back via recommendation from deliberate appointment. Feed economics also run on interruption—ads between clips, "Up Next," notifications—while ritual wants continuity: predictable schedule, unbroken experience. One monetizes detours; the other minimizes them. Optimizing for ritual implies a different mix: subscription over ads; loyalty over session extension.

Ritual builds loyalty to a creator; feed builds loyalty to the platform. From a platform's perspective, creator loyalty is dependency risk—the audience might follow elsewhere. Platform loyalty keeps viewers captive regardless of which creators are present. So ritual infrastructure grows where it's aligned (Discord, email, owned sites) and remains second-class wherever the feed is the business.

Go look where belonging is obvious and unpretentious. A Minecraft server is not just a game—it's a clubhouse with rules, lore, a clock people remember. Kids don't "tune in," they show up because their people are there. Discord repeats the shape. A standing voice room at a posted time. The same names in the sidebar. Mid-tier Twitch channels do it nightly. The streamer's cadence is the product. The chat is the room. The pattern holds across contexts—what changes is the wrapper, not the gravity.

In late 2020, the gap was obvious but nobody was building for it: kids outgrowing YouTube Kids' preschool fare but not ready for the main site's unmonitored chaos. Six-to-ten-year-olds who see themselves as eight-to-twelve. That developmental stage—where identity starts forming and kids want worlds they can inhabit, not just watch—had no good answer. YouTube couldn't officially admit the audience existed without confronting COPPA at scale. Platforms optimized for adults or toddlers. The middle was orphaned.

My cofounders and I tried to answer it with a prototype called superchannel—a kids-first, themed channel network built for 6–10. Not another feed. Themed channels that behaved like TV—a clock people could remember, a room we actually held, named bits that made the world legible, and participation that counted. Science kids. Craft kids. Gaming storytellers. We were trying to build cultural infrastructure around a passion that already exists, not just serve more content.

We built it with our own money. Simple mechanics: thematic cohesion so the world felt like itself; curated flow so the day had a shape—openers, middle beats, a closer that said see you tomorrow; community woven in from the start—votes that actually changed the next segment, fan work surfaced on the main run, a visible ladder from watcher to contributor. Identity mattered. Six-to-ten see themselves as eight-to-twelve. Talk down and they bounce. Meet the aspiration, hide the guardrails, they stay.

The hard part was safety without surveillance—age gates felt condescending and pushed kids toward less-safe spaces where they could pretend to be older. Heavy-handed moderation read as policing and made normal kid behavior feel criminal. We built a language system that swapped adult words for memorable pattern sounds—obvious to everyone in-world, harmless to everyone outside. Kids got the joke immediately. It became part of the culture, something they recognized as theirs. Light-touch threat detection ran in the background for grooming patterns and targeted cruelty. Human review on flags. No cops in the chat window.

Create and be seen was the other pillar. Kids wanted to remix and post. We gave them tools to do it inside the walls—save videos, remix clips, surface favorites—with status that came from contribution, not just views. We borrowed from Club Penguin's moderated play model and tried to push it further.

We shared it with small groups. The prototype was well received. Adults asked if we could build something similar for them—a way to follow creators they actually chose instead of whatever YouTube wanted to serve them that day. The need was real.

We went to raise money to build the actual product. Couldn't. The objections rhymed: kids' content is hard to monetize, YouTube Kids already exists, how will you get kids to go there? We had answers for one and two. Three—distribution, the cold start—is what kills most good ideas. We weren't successful fundraisers. Track record wasn't strong enough. Not well connected. Not from money ourselves. VCs don't fund what's right. They fund what fits. We were the similar thesis at the wrong time in the wrong cap table. People talk a good game about child safety—until money's on the line.

Five years later, the problem is worse. More kids, more hours, worse content, bigger concerns. The need we saw then is front-page now.

The lesson wasn't that ritual is a nice-to-have. The lesson was that the need was real, ritual was the right frame, but you need capital to reach the scale where the real fight begins. Five years later, the infrastructure is better. The need is louder. The distribution problem hasn't changed.

Anyone building this today still needs either a platform partnership that drives traffic or enough capital to survive the years it takes for word-of-mouth to compound. The distribution problem isn't technical. It's gravitational. Kids follow older kids, and older kids are already on the platforms that won the last war. You can build something better, safer, more coherent—and kids will still choose the place where their friends are. That's not about quality.

That's about where sessions start and social capital gets stored. Instagram's tablet opens to Reels, not your feed. You're watching before you choose, and the platforms are built to keep it that way.

Factory incentives fight you the whole way—feeds reward novelty and sameness at once, and they hand you the start, not the return. The feed doesn't just reward novelty; it manufactures sameness—rounded edges, familiar arcs, the safe middle that travels. Ritual cuts against that because a room remembers you for being specific. You can sprint for a while on volume. Then you burn out your team and train the audience to sample you instead of belong to you. Owning a room sounds like extra work. It is. It's also how a rented start turns into a durable return.

I worked with an advisor to Lee Asher when the fork appeared: become the face of a national pet-retail brand, or build owned products and keep the value inside the community. He had the option because of the audience he'd built—weekly fosters, adoption runs on a clock, live check-ins where names get read and miles get covered. The content points to action and the action loops back into the content—dogs placed, funds raised, the next run already posted. That's not just celebrity. It's a working rhythm the audience recognizes as theirs. Women who were pet parents and shared his passion for protecting animals showed up to his live events. They donate, transport, adopt, host meetups. That devotion created leverage. Petco came calling. Brand-deal money is fast and visible. Owned products are slow, margin-thin, and risky—white-label partners, authenticity questions, limits on future sponsor opportunities. He chose the brand deal. Smart choice. But the fact that he could choose at all? That came from the ritual, not the clip count. Parasocial at scale is cheap; affiliation is earned. The difference is whether people can act inside the room and be seen by name when they do.

JohnWallStreet built a smaller audience with outsized pull because the ritual runs on professional time. A reliable drop that hits before calls start. A voice that reads like a colleague, not a press release. Names and numbers you can carry into a meeting an hour later. Then the loop widens—Q&A threads that surface deal intel, meetups tied to tentpoles, a research product that turns the newsletter's language into the industry's shorthand. Readers cite pieces in decks. They forward them to partners. They show up live because that's where the nuance is. The cadence is the product and the room holds the practice. Growth moves from the inside out—operators inviting other operators because it saves time and sharpens decisions. People don't just consume it. They use it. They'll be back because the work runs better when they are, and because the room remembers them when they return.

The shift from attention to affiliation changes what matters. Attention is easy to rent. Affiliation is what you build and hold. When people see themselves in what you make, they don't just watch—they belong. That's not sentiment. That's the pattern that survives platform shifts and algorithm changes. Watch what platforms do next. They'll build "community features" that look like rooms but behave like feeds. They'll add badges and tiers and call it belonging. Money will reward the launch, not the

12 RITUAL & RETURN

outcome, because investors can't tell the difference between a feature that creates affiliation and one that fakes it long enough to juice a quarter.

The creators who see through this won't fight the platforms. They'll just hold the parts platforms can't replicate: the clock people trust, the room they actually control, the language that doesn't fit in a product spec. Everyone stacked tools until they felt like platforms; almost no one took responsibility for the room. The sticky parts are the opposite of tool-chase—they're what you own when everything else is rented.

What would work differently if you built superchannel today? The infrastructure gaps are smaller. Moderation tools are better. FAST channels proved there's appetite for curated lanes you can just put on and hang with. Roblox and Discord showed kids will commit to persistent spaces if the world feels like theirs. The unit economics are still harder than passive feeds, but the cost to build is lower. You'd still need a wedge—either a partnership with an established platform that drives traffic, or a cultural hook so strong that word-of-mouth becomes the engine. The former is the better bet. Both still require more capital and patience than most startups can sustain. The signal we read was right. The timing was early. The part we couldn't solve—getting kids to choose a new destination over the platforms they already live in—remains the hardest problem.

The mechanics repeat. A clock you keep even when you'd rather move it. A room you control when the feed looks away. Named pieces so recognition is instant. Participation tied to something that actually changes. Curation over chaos. Programming over dumping. Not old-school appointment TV, but something more ambient—a sense of there's always something good on without the pressure to decide what that is every time you sit down. The feeds amplify that. They don't replace it. The game moved from posting more to holding a place people recognize. Channels beat shows when the pressure to be everywhere turns into being somewhere on time.

You pay a toll whichever way you turn—push hard for the feed and you give up ownership, lock down control and you give up the first play. The goal isn't perfection, it's stickiness: accept discovery where it happens and hold the relationship somewhere that's yours. The durable parts are simple—the clock they remember, the room you can actually reach, the language that stitches fragments into a world.

A Minecraft movie opened to over $300 million worldwide—not because it was great cinema, but because kids showed up for a world they already belonged to. They participated, remixed, shared. Theatrical success isn't about mass appeal anymore. It's about emotional ownership. The room matters when the audience already has a relationship with what's inside it.

You can measure it without a religion. Same names at the same time. Opens that spike on the day you always send. Live rooms that refill without a blast. Comments that use your language without quoting you. Merch that sells because it carries membership, not because it carries a logo. None of that is mystical. It is repetitive, and that's the work. If the reflex shows up without a nudge, the ritual is working. Live sports showed the tell: the first play now fires from a platform row more than from a brand. Ritual is what keeps Sunday from getting swallowed by the suggestion engine.

The scarcity flipped. Content is infinite. Intimacy isn't. Private Discords and paid newsletters aren't distribution channels—they're clubhouses. Drop-in calls, members-only streams, live events that matter because you're in the room. People pay for the feeling of being in the right place with the right people, not just access to the content. CTV/FAST proved cadence still sells: the rows do discovery, but blocks do return. Slow is smooth when your clock is honest.

Brands have a role if they choose not to fight the physics. Sponsor the cadence, not the interruption. Pay to make the room bigger—cover the extra hour, the travel fund, the tool that keeps people together—and be remembered as the reason the good thing could happen again. Platforms do, too, if they admit the collective who. Recommend gatherings, not just titles. Show the cohort, not just the clip. Instrument continuity, not just time spent. If they won't, you still can, because the parts that matter most are the parts you hold.

EPILOGUE: THE NEXT SIGNAL_

I DIDN'T KNOW the shape of today when I first ran the Netflix numbers in 2004. I only knew behavior was moving faster than institutions, and that infrastructure would follow. That's been the spine of this book: the thing that looks like a content problem usually resolves into an infrastructure problem; the thing that looks like a talent problem usually resolves into a system problem. What we call disruption is often just delayed alignment.

Across the last twenty years, the pattern repeated enough times to be predictive. A new system lowers friction, a new behavior takes root, the incumbents dismiss it as a toy, then scramble to industrialize it after the audience has already voted with their time. Platforms arrive promising openness, then harden into their own gatekeeping. Creators arrive promising independence, then discover the subtle terms of service enforced by code. Audiences arrive for novelty, then stay for ritual. The energy starts at the edges and migrates, reluctantly, to the center. If you learn to read that migration early, you can see the next room before the door is installed. Recognize its shape and you'll see the turn before it arrives.

The present is loud with symptoms that look unrelated but are the same disease. Feeds that once felt like discovery now feel like reruns. Schedules exist again, only they're hidden inside home screens and push alerts. We chase reach that doesn't compound, mistaking the first minute for the next hour. Platforms tell us they're building for creators, and then adjust the payout dial a quarter-turn to protect their own margins. Brands tell us they want authenticity and then measure it like a pre-roll. None of this is shocking; it's what happens when a system optimizes for session length rather than belonging. Hits churn attention. Habits accumulate it. What we've been arguing for is a pivot from the first to the second.

We started with a question about attention—who controls what gets seen. That question led to power—who captures the value from visibility. Which forced us to look at infrastructure—the systems underneath that route everything. And at the end of that path was an uncomfortable realization: you became the product. Not just audiences. Creators too. Both sides provide unpaid inputs that platforms monetize. Twenty-five years ago, entertainment meant choosing from a grid. Then it meant controlling when you watched. Then it meant you could be the show. Now it means you—creator and viewer both—are the product. Each phase promised more freedom. Each phase delivered more extraction. That's not cynicism. It's the pattern.

We've also reached the point where the most valuable

output of these systems often isn't the show itself, or even the subscription. It's the behavioral trace. Some media and data companies are already generating high-margin revenue by licensing first-party viewing and purchase data to large language models and other AI systems. Wall Street loves it because it creates cash flow that's uncorrelated to ad spend or subscriber counts and doesn't depend on whether any particular show works. Your viewing exhaust —what you watched, when you paused, what you skipped, what you bought after—becomes training fuel for systems that have nothing to do with helping you find something better to watch tonight. The infrastructure doesn't just route you anymore. It harvests you, and sells what it learns to whoever can use it next.

If there's a single fulcrum on which the last phase turned, it's the home screen—the place where phone-native feeds and TV-native libraries now share the same glass, competing for the same living room. Not a page you visit, a place that visits you. Rows and rails that choose the route before taste can even weigh in. We used to talk about navigation like it was a user preference—tabs, menus, "where should search live?"—as if finding a thing would remain a voluntary act. The home screen rewired that. A session now begins the moment you arrive, which means discovery is an act of routing, not of browsing. The first decision is made for you, and your next two decisions are preloaded. What matters is less the title than the handoff: tile, trailer, placement—the order matters more than any single asset. In that world, "owning demand" is a myth. All that's left to own is the return.

Return is not a synonym for bingeing. It's trust

expressed as coming back. It's a viewer feeling that this space will meet them again with something they recognize and want, even when they don't know the name for it. Return has mechanics—honest cadence, legible vocabulary, a tone your audience can feel before they can articulate it—but it begins with a simple truth: the feed can start the session, but only structure keeps it. You can shout your way into someone's day; you have to design your way into someone's week. On the screen, that looks like what this book has been arguing toward: a channel people come back to on purpose, not by accident.

The most legible version of this shift shows up in how platforms and creators changed their posture once they stopped fighting yesterday's problem. Netflix is the case study everyone thinks they know, but look closer at where the company actually found leverage. Early on, the advantage wasn't studio relationships—it was a recommendation system that turned buried catalog into margin. Cinematch nudged viewers toward what was always available and often more profitable, which meant that surfacing the long tail wasn't a philosophical stance, it was a margin strategy. As streaming matured, the company's promotion logic followed the same pattern: fewer billboards and eventized trailers for the old first-touch, more tile science and microseeding aimed at session time. Netflix didn't win by producing better shows than everyone else, though it produced some great ones. It won by owning the route—reducing the distance between arrival and "play," and making each handoff feel inevitable. What looked like a better queue was really better routing: a default path through the grid that made "just hit play" feel safe. The first minute was defense; the next stretch was offense.

On the other side of the ecosystem, Mythical built the operator version of the same idea. Rhett & Link aren't a triumph of infinite novelty; they're a triumph of compounding return. What looks like personality is process—reliable rituals, teachable formats, a house style that translates across shows and seasons without turning into paste. They didn't just make more shows; they built a room you could walk into at 7 a.m. or 7 p.m. and know roughly how it would feel. The "studio" there isn't the building, it's the rules: what gets greenlit is what can be repeated without becoming rote, what can be staffed without losing the voice, what a sponsor fits into without sanding off edges. That's not a betrayal of authenticity; it's an articulation of it. Mythical didn't industrialize creativity so much as it professionalized return. The lesson isn't "become a corporation." It's "treat belonging like a system you can operate." If Netflix learned to seed like a creator, Mythical learned to program like a platform. Both moved from chasing the moment to owning the return, and both prospered because of it.

Once you accept that discovery sits upstream of you and will likely remain there, the decisions get simpler. You stop trying to own the entry point and start designing every touch to point toward the durable places you do control. That can be as prosaic as email and text and Discord, or as ambitious as your own channel presence on devices where your audience actually lives. The specifics will change with the tools; the posture won't. Distributed discovery, owned relationship. The feed can introduce you to a million strangers in an afternoon. Only your structure convinces a few thousand to come back on purpose.

Underneath the rhetoric, the economics are already voting for organization over volume. Platform-side ad systems will continue to reward whatever keeps the session alive, and open-market inventory will continue to look cheap when it can't prove return. Premium isn't a synonym for expensive production; it's a synonym for predictable behavior. Buyers pay for a cohort that comes back, not just a spike that photographs well. When you can demonstrate that your viewers persist, price holds. When you can't, price drifts. That's why "creator funds" and "bonus pools" feel generous for a quarter and thin by the year: they're not built on persistence; they're built on headlines. The money that stays attached to you is the money that can forecast you.

People sometimes hear this as a call to abandon platforms, go pure independence, wall yourself off from the algorithm. That's not what the evidence suggests. The next signal isn't isolation; it's orchestration. The system already routes viewers through a thousand side doors a day; your work is to turn any one of those doors into a room. The room can be small without being fragile. If you do that well, the platform feels less like a god and more like a utility. You stop praying for the right recommendation and start planning for the next return.

This is also where the old language of community misleads us. Affiliation isn't a community feature; it's gravity. The comments under a video matter less as a wall of text than as a signal that a conversation can continue somewhere that isn't rented by the hour. The switch flips when your audience recognizes the house they're in. That comes from words and tone and expectations repeated enough to become muscle memory. You don't have to name the rules for them to work. You just have to keep them.

If the last chapter sounded like an argument for ritual, this one is the matching argument for architecture. Ritual gives people reasons to come back; architecture gives them places to land. The two reinforce each other in a loop that looks suspiciously like the old broadcast model, except the center of gravity moved from show to channel to operator. Syndication is the right metaphor, but its nouns got swapped. The home screen is the broadcaster. The "buyer" is a recommendation row that believes you can keep someone in session. The "episode" is your channel itself, if the system thinks the route through it will hold. That change, quiet as it looks, flips a century of assumptions. You don't sell discrete units of programming to a schedule; you prove that your schedule routes programming into a habit. The catalog matters, but the grid matters more.

Everything exacts a cost. If you optimize for speed inside a feed, you'll narrow into sameness. If you optimize for continuity outside it, you'll trade away some top-of-funnel sugar. If you design a brand people can spot blindfolded, you'll occasionally lose a trend that wants to dress you in borrowed clothes. The point isn't to dodge the trade-offs but to choose them. When you choose them on purpose, your errors become experiments instead of accidents. You can correct a posture. You can't correct a prayer.

The predictable objection here is that all of this sounds

like a plan for large players and "studios," not for people. But the bias toward scale is mostly a storytelling habit. The inputs that matter are human-sized: a cadence you can keep, rules your collaborators can learn without a memo, a simple way for a viewer to know where to find you next time. Operators who look "big" usually got there by getting those small things right, then stacking them. The magic isn't capital. It's continuity.

When I say "the next signal," I don't mean a new social app that changes everyone's phone background. I mean infrastructure that treats operators as operators, not as anonymous supply. That can be as unglamorous as a ledger that finally reconciles a brand campaign across five surfaces without someone hand-entering screenshots, or as welcome as a device-level identity that lets a family tell a service, "This is the Tuesday profile"—and have it stick across rooms and screens. It might look like smarter bundling: fewer logins, fewer broken links, where the product being sold is the reduction of cognitive load, not content sprawl. It might look like a discovery layer that doesn't pretend to know your true self and instead asks the simple, accurate question, "Who are you right now—and how long do you have?" That's the identity-over-interface move in practice: treat the same person as many whos across a week, not one averaged profile. The point isn't to guess the winner. It's to recognize the form it will take: less spectacle, more alignment.

We've been here before. In 2004, the obvious story said people loved owning DVDs. The real story said they loved the experience the disc temporarily made possible. Streaming wasn't a revolution in taste; it was the removal of steps between intent and play. Today's obvious story says audiences love infinite feeds and atomic clips and microtrend velocity. The real story says they love not being lost. As the pipes get wider and the choices proliferate, the value of a trusted route increases, not decreases. The trick isn't to build the route with a louder sign. It's to build it with fewer wrong turns.

I don't know which companies will embody that or which ones will just tweet about it. I don't know which logos will be on the remote and which ones will be behind the scenes. But I know what the winners will share. They'll reduce the distance between arrival and understanding. They'll make return the unit of design. They'll move identity out of the marketing deck and into the interface, not as a profile picture but as a promise about what happens next. And, quietly, they'll design every lane and room around the same test you've seen throughout this book: who can sit in this without flinching?

What came after Blockbuster wasn't "better stores." What came after "TV on the internet" wasn't more TV. What comes after feed-era creation isn't a shinier feed. It's a layer that reconciles what people already do with how they actually want to live. When behavior moves, infrastructure follows, and new rooms get built. You won't see the next ones first in a press release. You'll hear them sideways: a twelve-year-old in a living room saying, "Just put on the gaming lane," a group chat that keeps returning to the same link because "this is our thing now." The signal will show up as relief before it reads as innovation—less hunting, more returning; less shouting, more knowing where to go.

By the time someone gives it a name, the habit will already exist, and the room will already feel familiar. Twenty years ago I learned to separate direction from timing. The direction is clear again. The timing will announce itself the moment the audience recognizes the room as theirs. The room is ready.

ACKNOWLEDGMENTS_

This book exists because people shared their time and perspective along the way.

Some of that came during the writing itself. My deepest thanks to Harry Poloner, Courtney Cook, Michael Cerda, Eric Goldstein, Jason Krebs, Jim Louderback, Nathan Pettijohn, and my brother, Darrell Cross, who read early drafts, asked hard questions, and helped me find my way.

Most of it came from the colleagues and mentors who taught me how to see the patterns—the ones who let me watch the system in motion and argued with me when I got it wrong. You're in the stories themselves. You know who you are.

I also want to thank my mom and dad for their support and curiosity about my wandering professional life, even when they never really understood what I did.

Monica, Tina, and Lucas gave me the support and belief I needed to finish it.

—DC

Los Angeles, California. December, 2025.

ABOUT THE AUTHOR_

Darren Cross has spent two decades spotting media shifts before they became obvious. He began in equity research, building early models for Netflix and arguing for streaming when most of the industry waved it off—and that habit of reading the signal has defined his career.

He's worked at the center of the transition from broadcast to platform: Wedbush (analyzing Netflix pre-streaming), ClickStar (day-and-date releases backed by Morgan Freeman and Intel), Fandango (as mobile made the internet always-on), Maker Studios (as creators became an economic force, later acquired by Disney), and Unreel (scaling a white-label OTT platform powering hundreds of apps).

His advisory work spans streaming and creator infrastructure: Amagi (CTV), MediaPress (metadata), CreatorIQ (creator analytics), Jukin Media (viral IP), and GoldieBlox (kids' media).

Today, Darren splits his time between distllr—a fractional-executive firm that helps high-velocity teams bridge strategy and execution—and SGNL, a creator-powered syndication layer for connected TV that builds the brand-backed, creator-led channels described in this book. He holds a JD and an MBA, is a member of the California Bar, and writes about the changing rules of media, attention, and identity.

No One Planned This is his first book.

www.ingramcontent.com/pod-product-compliance
Lightning Source LLC
Chambersburg PA
CBHW020540030426
42337CB00013B/921